A
NATIONAL
AWAKENING

Robin Mathews
and the Struggle for
Canadian Identity

A
NATIONAL
AWAKENING

Robin Mathews
and the Struggle for
Canadian Identity

Edited by
Joyce Wayne

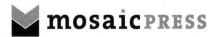 mosaicPRESS

Library and Archives Canada Cataloguing in Publication

Title: A national awakening : Robin Mathews & the struggle for Canadian identity / edited by Joyce Wayne.

Names: Wayne, Joyce, 1951- editor.

Identifiers: Canadiana (print) 20240339207
Canadiana (ebook) 2024033941X

ISBN 9781771617529 (softcover) | ISBN 9781771617536 (PDF)
ISBN 9781771617543 (EPUB) | ISBN 9781771617550 (Kindle)

Subjects: LCSH: Mathews, Robin, 1931-2023–Influence. | LCSH: Mathews, Robin, 1931-2023–Criticism and interpretation. | LCSH: Nationalism–Canada. | LCSH: Politicians–Canada–Biography. | LCSH: College teachers–Canada–Biography. | CSH: Authors, Canadian (English)–Biography. | LCGFT: Biographies.

Classification: LCC FC97 .N38 2024
DDC 320.540971–dc23

Published by Mosaic Press, Oakville, Ontario, Canada, 2024.
MOSAIC PRESS, Publishers
www.Mosaic-Press.com

Printed and bound in Canada.

MOSAIC PRESS
1252 Speers Road, Units 1 & 2, Oakville, Ontario, L6L 2X4 (905)-825-2130
info@mosaic-press.com • www.mosaic-press.com

For Esther and the Mathews family

CONTRIBUTORS

DUNCAN CAMERON graduated with a B.A. from the University of Alberta and received his doctorate from the University of Paris I (Paris-Sorbonne). He taught political science for over 30 years, most recently at Simon Fraser University. Cameron was the editor of the monthly *Canadian Forum* magazine from 1989 to 1998. He is the author, co-author, editor or co-editor of 11 books including *Ethics and Economics* (with Gregory Baum), *The Other Macdonald Report* (with Daniel Drache), *The Free Trade Papers*, *The Free Trade Deal*, *Canada Under Free Trade* (with Mel Watkins) and *Constitutional Politics* (with Miriam Smith). He is the president emeritus of the Canadian Centre for Policy Alternatives and was a weekly columnist for rabble.ca

SUSAN CREAN is a writer of eight books, one co-authored with Marcel Rioux and published in French and English. (*Deux Pays Pour Vivre/Two Nations*). She has been a teacher, consultant and editor, and is a former chair of the Writers Union of Canada (1991/2). She was the first Executive Secretary Canadian Artists' Representation in the early 1970s, Distinguished Visitor and guest lecturer at the University of Alberta in 1986, and that year was appointed the first Maclean-Hunter Chair in Creative non-Fiction at the Department of Creative Writing, University of British Columbia. Her book *The Laughing One: A Journey to Emily Carr* was short-listed for the Governor General's Literary Award for non-fiction in 2001 and won the Hubert Evans Non-fiction Award. She taught feature writing at Ryerson University's School of Journalism between 2000 and 2007, and was founding co-chair of the Creators' Rights Alliance (CRA/ADC) in 2002. She also served as a director of CANCOPY (now Access Copyright) between 1992 and 1995, and similarly a director of Native Earth Performing Arts between 2001 and 2010. She remains a long-time member of the editorial board of *This Magazine*.

MISAO DEAN is a professor in the English Department at the University of Victoria, where she has taught since 1989. She is a specialist in the Canadian novel and in Canadian travel literature, and has published many academic articles on Canadian literature and culture. Her most recent book is *Inheriting a Canoe Paddle* (U of T. Press, 2013). Her MA thesis was supervised by Robin Mathews, and she was a volunteer and a paid staff member for Steel Rail Publishing and the Great Canadian Theatre Company during 1980–1982.

DANIEL DRACHE is Professor Emeritus and Senior Research Fellow of the Robarts Centre for Canadian Studies, York University. He has published widely on Canadian political economy, North American integration, globalization and counter-publics. For more about his research and writing, see https://danieldrache.com In the 1970s he shared many public platforms with Robin Mathews on the Canadianization of the university. His latest book, *Has Populism Won? The War on Liberal Democracy* is published by ECW Toronto, 2023. (co-written with Marc Froese).

ALVIN FINKEL is professor emeritus of Canadian History at Athabasca University. In retirement, he is the nearly full-time president of the Alberta Labour History Institute. He is a prolific author of monographs, textbooks, book chapters, academic articles, and articles in popular magazines and newspapers. His books include seven editions of the two-volume *History of the Canadian Peoples*; *Our Lives: Canada After 1945*; *Social Policy and Practice in Canada: A History*; *Working People in Alberta: A History*; *Compassion: A Global History of Social Policy*; *The Social Credit Phenomenon in Alberta*; *The Chamberlain-Hitler Collusion*; and the soon to be published *Humans: A History*.

BILL LAW co-founded GCTC with Robin Mathews and two fellow students. He served as artistic director from 1975–1978. Following two years as editor at James Lorimer in Toronto he joined the CBC in Edmonton where he was a producer and executive producer in Radio Current Affairs and Radio Arts. While in Edmonton, he was instrumental in unionising radio producers across Canada. He left the CBC in 1992 moving to the UK where he was a senior broadcast journalist at the BBC. Serving as a reporter and documentary maker, he worked extensively in the Middle East and North Africa. He also reported from the Americas, Africa, Afghanistan and Pakistan. Before leaving the BBC in 2014, Law was the corporation's Gulf analyst. Currently, he is the editor of the daily arabdigest.org. newsletter and presenter of the weekly Arab Digest podcast.

SINCLAIR ROBINSON was born in 1943 in Palmerston, Ontario. He attended a one-room school and then did Grade 9 at Norwell District High School in Palmerston. When he was fourteen, he moved from the farm with his family to London, Ontario. He graduated from London South Collegiate Institute, and then did an Honours BA in French and German at the University of Western Ontario. There followed four years of post-graduate studies in linguistics and translation at Rochester, NY, Strasbourg and Laval. He was hired by Carleton in 1969 and taught in the Department of French for forty years. He taught language courses at various levels, courses in French linguistics, on Canadian French in particular, and translation courses. He was Chair of the Department for eight years and guided the Department through some turbulent years. He was involved in university governance at various levels. Besides the publications mentioned in this article, he was active in language course development in the department and published numerous translations in various fields.

PAT SMART is Chancellor's Professor Emerita at Carleton University and the author of several volumes on Quebec literature and visual arts. Her *Hubert Aquin agent double: La dialectique de l'art et du pays dans "Prochain Episode" et "Trou de mémoire"* (Presses de l'Université de Montréal, 1973) was the first critical work published on Aquin. In 1988, her feminist analysis of Quebec literature *Ecrire dans la maison du Père: l'émergence du féminin dans la tradition littéraire du Québec* (Québec/Amérique) was awarded the Governor General's Literary Award, and in 1998 her *Les Femmes du Refus global* was a finalist for the same award. In 2005 she published a critical edition of Claire Martin's memoir *Dans un gant de fer*. Her study of Quebec women's autobiographical writings *De Marie de l'Incarnation à Nelly Arcan : se dire, se faire par l'écriture intime* (Éditions du Boréal, 2014) won the Prix Jean-Éthier Blais, the Gabrielle Roy Prize and the Ottawa Book Award, and was a finalist for Ontario's Trillium Award. Her own translation of this book, *Writing Herself Into Being: Quebec Women's Autobiographical Writings from Marie de l'Incarnation to Nelly Arcan* (McGill-Queen's University Press) was published in 2017. She was elected to the Royal Society of Canada in 1991 and became a Member of the Order of Canada in 2004.

ERROL SHARPE was born and raised on a small farm in P.E.I. in 1940 and is a publisher at Fernwood Publishing. He holds a BA in Political Science and Literature from Saint Dunstan's University and an MA in Atlantic Canadian

Studies from Saint Mary's University. In 1976 he authored *A People's History of Prince Edward Island*. In 1978 he founded Fernwood Books, a sales company primarily selling books to the academic market for a number of Canadian publishing companies. In 1982 he co-founded Garamond Press and founded Fernwood Publishing in 1991. He is the co-author, with Stacey Byrne, of *In Pursuit of Justice: Just Us Coffee Roasters Co-op and the Fairtrade Movement* and, with Kent Martin, Sharpe compiled *Milton Acorn: The People's Poet*.

DONALD SMITH, Professor Emeritus, chair of the Department of French for two terms at Carleton University, has published numerous articles and 17 books dealing with Québec French, literature and singers, most notably *L'Écrivain devant son oeuvre* (interviews with Québec and Acadian writers, translated into English as *Voices of Deliverance*), *Dictionary of Canadian French* (co-authored with the linguist Sinclair Robinson), *Gilles Vigneault, conteur et poète, Jacques Godbout: du roman au cinéma*, and *D'une nation à l'autre* (published in translation as *Beyond Two Solitudes*). He was also for many years responsible for interviews in the Québec literary review *Lettres québécoises*. As an editor for the publisher Québec Amérique, he was the director of the series "Littérature d'Amérique; traduction" in which major English-Canadian authors (including Robertson Davies, Stephen Leacock, W.O. Mitchell and Lucy Maud Montgomery) as well as Jack Kerouac were published in French. He is now writing articles in Catalan comparing the Catalan and Québec nations as "countries within the country" and has published in collaboration one book in Catalan and another in French on the North Catalonian poet and songwriter from France, Joan Paul Giné.

JOYCE WAYNE studied English with Robin Mathews at Carleton University in the 1970s. She was an editor at *Quill & Quire*, Director of Non-fiction at McClelland & Stewart and the publicist for James Lorimer and Co. Joyce taught journalism at Sheridan College where she launched the Canadian Journalism for Internationally Trained Writers program. Her novels include *Last Night of the World* and *The Cook's Temptation*. Joyce's essay "All the Kremlin's Men" was chosen for Best Canadian Essays 2021.

TABLE OF CONTENTS

INTRODUCTION

By Joyce Wayne

W hat would Robin Mathews think if he scanned his morning newspaper for the day's leading stories, reviewed his email, or listened to the CBC? The Canada he fought for is disappearing. Economically, politically and culturally, the country is in decline and, in certain ways, has been so since the 1988 Free Trade Election. With that Progressive Conservative victory, Prime Minister Brian Mulroney managed to usher in another majority government, which would sign off on the Canada-U.S. Free Trade Agreement. For Mathews and the group of students, teachers, artists and rowdy bands of activists who gathered around him, the fight for an independent Canada was beginning to fade.

This collection of essays, many by writers who worked closely with Mathews, focuses on the Ottawa years between 1968 and 1984. In 1969, fresh from a 2-year sojourn in the U.K. and France, Mathews and his colleague James Steele published *The Struggle for Canadian Universities*, a dossier revealing the dearth of Canadian subject matter taught in our universities and the surprisingly minuscule number of Canadian professors who were being hired to teach here. Their book caught the attention of politicians, professors, students, and university administrators nationwide. The media focused on Mathews as he lamented the lack of Canadian course content and the erosion of the distinct Canadian identity he cherished.

National Awakening: Robin Mathews and the Struggle for Canadian Identity is a close look at the intellectual history of that period, those who supported Mathews and those who were disappointed by or disagreed with him, and the political and cultural change he exerted on the country. Pat Smart, Sinclair Robinson and Donald Smith discuss how Mathews initiated a report revealing the scarcity of content about Canada in French departments across the country. Duncan Cameron recollects Mathews' early days as a professor at the University of Alberta, where he began his journey as a radical and as a public speaker. In "Robin Mathews and the Canadianization of Trade Unions," Alvin Finkel recounts Mathews' work with Kent Rowley and Madeline Parent's Confederation of Canadian Unions (CCU). Bill Law talks about the growing pains of Ottawa's Great Canadian Theatre Company (GCTC), of which Robin and Bill were among the founders. Misao Dean's critique of Mathews' literary work pulls no punches as she dissects the highs and lows of his creative endeavours. In Susan Crean's "The Robin Mathews Project: Knowing Canada," she recounts the early days of activism among cultural workers. To conclude, Errol Sharpe describes the radical activist that Mathews was and how his ideas remain relevant to current contentious issues sizzling in the country.

During this period, Mathews' protestations struck a chord with scores of others, primarily left nationalists in the Waffle, a splinter group of the New Democratic Party, as well as with small extreme radical parties, the Canadian Liberation Movement being the most representative of Mathews' thinking. Artists, novelists, playwrights, poets and his students were often among Mathews' followers.

Yet, nationalism went against the grain for many, beginning with Prime Minister Pierre Trudeau, an ardent internationalist and staunch opponent of Quebec's independence. Among the organized Left, the opposition to Mathews' nationalism was often the most vehement. NDP leader David Lewis, also an internationalist, emphatically opposed Mathews' support for the burgeoning Canadian union movement. Lewis' New Democratic Party depended on the support of U.S.-headquartered unions, the UAW and the United Steelworkers. Among some radical professors and their students, Canadian nationalism was viewed as a bourgeois luxury, having nothing to do with the Marxist concept of "the primary contradiction" between labour and capital. Mathews never succumbed to this doctrine, believing that it was the struggle between nationalism and imperialism that overshadowed all other considerations.

As Daniel Drache writes in the opening essay of this book, "Robin Mathews was a man for his times, rabble-rouser, shit disturber, provocateur, patriot, silver-tongued orator, nationalist, a fearless in-your-face public intellectual butting heads with Canada's elites." Either soliciting undying devotion from his followers or intense enmity from his opponents, Mathews rode the 1970s and early 1980s wave of what was Canada's attempt at political and cultural sovereignty and economic independence from the U.S. until he and his wife Esther moved from Ottawa to Vancouver. In 1984, Robin resigned as an English professor at Carleton University, leaving behind a record of his political career's most influential ideas and actions as a Canadian nationalist, radical activist, public intellectual and media personality.

In these eight original essays, today's public intellectuals paint a portrait, not only of an avidly committed person but of a complex personality who demanded loyalty from his followers at the same time as he supported their artistic, academic and political successes. For a time, I was one of those, mesmerized by Mathews' energy and determination while wishing to break free of his influence and intractability. With his passing in April 2023, at the age of 92, Robin Mathews left behind a body of work and a host of Canadians who will forever be touched by his generosity of spirit and his enduring love for this country.

Joyce Wayne
Oakville, Ontario

ROBIN MATHEWS:
CULTURAL ACTIVIST, NATIONALIST INFLUENCER AND AGENDA-SETTER

By Daniel Drache

Native Born vs. Foreign Imports

Robin Mathews was a man for his times, rabble-rouser, shit disturber, provocateur, patriot, silver-tongued orator, nationalist, a fearless in-your-face public intellectual butting heads with Canada's elites. He had just published *The Struggle for Canadian Universities: A Dossier*, with James Steele, his colleague and close collaborator in the late 60s, that transformed Mathews into a national figure campaigning to Canadianize English Canada's universities. At the time, the term 'Canadianization' was a highly charged concept. It was synonymous with controversial faculty hiring practices, core curriculum, American professors taking jobs from qualified Canadians, national identity and Ottawa's refusal to correct this failure of planning.[1]

In the late 60s, many Canadians were alarmed by American interests that had come to dominate the Canadian psyche and national mood. The publication of John Porter's *Vertical Mosaic* several years earlier was an intellectual bombshell and bestseller forcing Canadians to take a hard look at their institutions and the interlocking power networks of the dominant elites in education, politics and the economy. Porter's empirical analysis of Canada's power elites turbocharged public interest in Mathews' and Steele's explosive dossier on the American takeover of Canada's university system.

The exact number of American ex-pats can never be known accurately because faculty composition was considered such a low priority that very little data was collected by Canada's universities or governments federally or

---

[1] The focus of the Canadianization university movement is English Canada based with some significant linkages with Québec. Québec nationalism has its own separate iteration, narrative and history. The 'two solitudes' divide is evident in Paul Grayson, "Struggles About Canadianization In Anthropology and Sociology", CAUT – December 2005 and in much of the literature on Canadian nationalism.

1

provincially.[2] In departments like sociology, anthropology, philosophy, and political science, Canadian professors often found themselves in the minority and passed over for full-time positions.[3]

Mathews' and Steele's dossier commanded a wide readership because it made a detailed, empirically driven case that Canadian universities faced an unparalleled crisis of governance. What drew many to support them is that they presented a tightly argued case, heavily researched from original data, demonstrating that qualified Canadians were being denied opportunities for positions in their own country.

At the time, it helped a lot that they were not a lone voice in the wilderness. There were many other nationalists speaking and writing about corporate takeovers, foreign control of Canada's trade union movement, the news media, book publishing, and mass culture.[4] Walter Gordon's *Storm Signals New Economic Policies for Canada*, David Godfrey's *From Gordon to Watkins to You, Documentary: The Battle For Control Of Our Economy*, and Kari Levitt's *Silent Surrender: The Multinational Corporation In Canada* commanded a wide, popular readership. During two intense decades, Robin exerted an outsized influence and presence in these debates and controversies which led to profound changes in Canada's academic culture for new hires in the professoriate ranks and, what he termed, 'promoting cultural literacy' as a foundational principle of curriculum development.[5]

---

[2] Kim Richard Nossal has collected some very useful data for hirings in international relations in Canadian departments and it allows us to gain a good idea of the scale of hirings in the more recent period as well as an approximation of hires during a period of rapid University expansion in the earlier decades. See "Homegrown IR: the Canadianization of International Relations", *Journal of Canadian Studies* Vol. 35, No. 1. Spring 2000. Bryan D. Palmer, *Canada 1960s The Irony Of Identities In The Rebellious Era*, University of Toronto Press, 2009.

[3] See Robert Brym's account of hiring in the U of T's Department of sociology, "Our First 50 Years: A Note on the University of Toronto's Department of Sociology, *The Canadian Journal of Sociology / Cahiers canadiens de sociologie*, vol 51 no.3, 2014. Without a thorough audit we will never know the precise number of American professors given jobs in Canada.

[4] Many of the leading figures were economists including Kari Levitt, Abe Rotstein, Mel Watkins, Cy Gonick, Marjorie Cohen. Others were cultural activists/ publishers including Jack McClelland, James Lorimer, and David Godfrey, each of whom played a critical role in disseminating the ideas, studies, edited volumes and policy studies of the nationalist movement. See Ian Lumsden's highly relevant edited volume., *Close the 49th Parallel ETC: The Americanization of Canada*, University of Toronto Press, 1970. It remains an excellent sampling of nationalist ideas and outlooks from this era.

[5] If you knew Robin or shared a public platform with him, it was an unforgettable experience. He was not your stereotypical Canadian low-key public presenter. He was

Mathews' and Steele's examination of course curricula and syllabi across the country revealed the failure of Canadian universities to have a core curriculum with readily available material that addressed Canada's cultural needs. There were so few courses on Canadian literature, working-class history, feminism, Québec, First Nations, poverty, immigrant communities, environmentalism, foreign policy, and Canadian intellectual and political thought, to name only some of the glaring omissions. At the time, you might have thought that social science was an American import with a few Canadian examples thrown in for good measure. Or if the prof. was a former Oxford don, the teaching material might have looked like a leftover of a white imperial elite education. You wouldn't be mistaken.[6]

Dennis Lee in his magisterial essay, "Cadence, Country Silence: Writing In Colonial Space", said it best, warning that Canadians were a people disconnected from who we were becoming and overpowered by a legacy of cultural crippling silence about our lived experience. He wrote:

> The colonized people are full of unfocused resentment, which it directs against itself. Resentment because its citizens are unable to partake in the life of their country with dignity or self-respect—since they don't even own it; unfocused because it has been bred into them that they are innately inferior, they have somehow brought this deprivation on themselves. "Canadians never recognize anything good if it is their own." "Canadians will never risk money in their own country." "Canadians are a bore." It is from put-down remarks such as these that the colonial must fashion his sense of worth and identity. So far as that goes, the criticisms are usually true. But they do not describe anything innate; they describe the defence mechanisms of a colonized people. Nevertheless, they are taken up and recited by that people in a frenzy of self-hatred. Nobody runs down Canada more than the Canadians.[7]

The Crisis of Numbers

We don't know if Robin believed he could really win this battle defeating the debilitating effects of our colonial psychology. In the 1961 census, data

---

brash and passionate about the future of Canada. In this better version of himself he had a lot of practical ideas about long-term solutions to the Canadian University system. In other arenas he was a polarizing figure.

[6] 6 Dennis Lee, "Cadence, Country, Silence: Writing In Colonial Space", Boundary 2 Vol. 3, No. 1, A Canadian Issue (Autumn, 1974), pp. 151-168 (18 pages).Published By Duke University Press.

[7] Op.cit.

showed that the proportion of Canadians on faculty was almost 75 percent. Only a decade later the number of Canadians in faculties of arts and science in some 15 universities had dropped to 49 percent. In many departments Canadian faculty were in the minority.

When The *Struggle for Canadian Universities* was published, it triggered a countrywide policy debate about the discriminatory hiring practices by Canadian academics. The dossier revealed that in 1969 only 55 percent of the faculty teaching in Canadian universities were Canadians. Departments such as sociology and anthropology were in crisis mode. According to Mathews and Steele, only 39 percent of sociologists and 29 percent of anthropologists were Canadian citizens. A few years later only about 50 percent of all graduate students in departments such as sociology were Canadians.

The situation became so dire that a group of angry, young nationalist-minded graduate students in the University of Toronto's Department of Sociology passed a motion demanding policies to find qualified Canadian applicants, stop hiring non-Canadians, ensure that 75 percent of graduate students were Canadian and that research funding give preference to Canadians studying in Canada.[8] When it came to hiring new faculty, Canadians were not interviewed, jobs were not advertised and often Americans were hired directly over the phone from the U.S. Mathews and Steele were not talking about one department in one isolated Canadian university, but a nationwide systemic university crisis.

Foreign scholars have always been welcomed in Canadian universities both as faculty and administrators. Back then, Canadian hiring practices had long been controversial. During the late 30s and 40s, Harold Innis, Canada's distinguished international political economist, was passed over as chair of the prestigious Department of Political Economy at the University of Toronto.[9] Innis wasn't an isolated case. Canada's universities were still in thrall to their British colonial origins and ex-pats from Oxford and Cambridge were repeatedly recruited for the top jobs.[10] Yet, the hiring politics of the 60s that

---

[8]   Paul Grayson, op.cit.

[9]   The Chair of the prestigious Department of Political Economy always had been held by an imported Brit until University of Toronto relented and appointed Harold Innis as the first Canadian chair, *Harold Innis: Staples, Markets, And Cultural Change, Selected Essays* edited by Daniel Drache, McGill Queens, 1993.

[10]   Innis was finally appointed Chair some years later.

confronted Mathews were very different in scope and scale from previous decades.[11]

For instance, Mathews and Steele found that at Laurentian University's political science department, only a one-half course was offered in Canadian government. Its geography department offered no courses in Canadian geography. It is still shocking to discover that its English department offered none in Canadian literature. Mathews and Steele collected massive amounts of evidence by examining university calendars and culling data from Statistics Canada and other agencies. They also carried on a voluminous correspondence with academics all over the country who wrote to Mathews documenting the opaque and arbitrary hiring practices of an 'old boys' network at their universities.[12] From this correspondence, it is possible to see the groundswell of support their Canadianization campaign received from Canadian academics across the country even though many weren't brave enough to support them publicly. Hundreds of these letters are part of the Mathews archives now open to the public at the National Archives in Ottawa.

The Calamitous Carleton Meeting

At Carleton University where Mathews and Steeles taught, their campaign started disastrously when their 1968 proposals for fundamental change were massively rejected by their colleagues in a special meeting of the Carleton University Academic Staff Association by 138 votes to 2.[13] In a second vote, the count was 138 to 5.

Mathews and Steele presented five remedial motions to treat Canadian citizens equitably when Canadians were becoming a minority in many departments. They demanded that over time, two-thirds of the faculty would be Canadian citizens. They also demanded that Canadian citizenship be required for all top administrative appointments. In terms of new hires, they called for job vacancies to be advertised and require an open search competition. They also demanded that their university gather information about the citizenship

11 James Steele and Robin Mathews, "Canadianization Revisited: A Comment on Cormier's "The Canadianization Movement in Context", *The Canadian Journal of Sociology* / Cahiers canadiens de sociologie, Autumn, 2006, Vol. 31, No. 4 (Autumn, 2006), pp. 491-508
12 Mathews and Steele, op. cit.
13 Robin Mathews and James Steele, ed., *The Struggle For Canadian Universities: A Dossier*, Toronto, New Press 1969. Jeffrey Cormier, *The Canadianization Movement: Emergence, Survival and Success*, University of Toronto Press 2004.

composition of the faculty. Finally, they made a special point directed to the Canadian Association of University teachers to collect information about the citizenship status of faculty teaching in Canadian universities. To that end the goal was to "strive as a general policy to employ Canadians of excellence in each department.[14] Even 50 years later, we can see the long tail of their impact on university hiring practices.

Who Were the Activists in Mathews' Army of Supporters?

Between 1969 and 1972 Mathews, by himself or with Steele, spoke at countless teach-ins about Canada's University crisis at many universities and colleges across Canada. They spoke at the University of Victoria, the University of British Columbia, Simon Fraser University, Calgary University, the University of Alberta, the University of Saskatchewan, the University of Manitoba, the University of Toronto, York University, Queen's University, Seneca College, Ontario Institute for Studies In Education, the University of Windsor, McGill University, Bishops University, Dawson College, Sir George Williams University, the University of New Brunswick, Mount Allison University, Dalhousie, and Memorial University. They also appeared frequently on radio and television and were interviewed dozens of times in the print media on the discriminatory hiring crisis in Canada's universities. They became public figures with a very loud public megaphone and a powerful message.

Mathews' campaign was different from the other nationalist movements of the time. It was not membership-based nor was it attached to any political party. Rather, it was an assemblage of nationalists, student activists, academics, writers and concerned citizens. At first, they were overshadowed by English Canada's nationalist movements such as the Waffle Movement inside the NDP and the Committee for An Independent Canada, a newly organized group of public intellectuals, economists, politicians and educators. These groups were better organized and financed, but Mathews was more successful in politicizing the issue of university hiring practices and curriculum reform to a large receptive Canadian public of universities, faculty and administrators across Canada, particularly the highly organized and mobilized student movement.

---

[14] James Steele and Robin Mathews, "the universities: takeover of the mind" in Ian Lumsden, op. cit. p. 177.

It's possible in hindsight to see how his framing of hiring practices became the jumping-off point for the Commission on Canadian Studies chaired by Tom Symons, formerly president of Trent University. Symons said: "As things now stand there are few other countries in the world with a developed postsecondary system that pay as little attention to the study of their own culture, problems and circumstances in the University".[15]

Governments Get Involved

Most of the Symons Report's 1000 recommendations were disregarded by governments. In many respects, the Symons report was a grand gesture but a major disappointment. On the critical issue of the responsibilities of university administrators to address the influx of American professors, it broke no new ground. It had little positive to recommend. On the central importance of citizenship to the future development of Canadian studies and university hiring practices, the Symons report was a huge let-down. It said almost next to nothing about the responsibilities of university administrators to hire Canadians, to advocate an affirmative action program or about the critical importance of citizenship as a condition of employment in job searches. [16]

From another angle, Abraham Rotstein came much closer to the truth when he wrote: "Of all peoples on earth, Canadians are least able to understand the process of Americanization. America is a total environment: it envelops us as a mist, penetrating every sphere of our cultural, political, economic and social environment. For that very reason, we seem to feel powerless, unwilling and unable to achieve the perspective necessary for an appraisal of our situation. It sometimes seems superfluous to ask what should

---

[15]   T.H.B.Symons, Chair, *To Know Ourselves, Report Of The Commission On Canadian Studies*, AUCC, 1976

[16]   That said, The Symons report gave a blast of energy to establish Canadian studies programs in many universities. In some universities, Canadian studies programs were established after much handwringing, but the results were often uneven and disappointing. At the international level, newly established Canadian studies programs funded academic visits by Indian, German, Chinese, Argentinian, Mexican, Italian, Israeli and Brazilian scholars. Hundreds of foreign scholars organized Canadian studies programs and centres in their own countries. Canadian academics participated across the globe in conferences, academic exchanges and visits. Later the Harper government recklessly defunded dozens of programs including Canadian studies in its neoliberal drive to downsize the role of the federal state.

be done about the Americanization of this country as it is to ask what should be done about the weather."[17]

With so much contradictory evidence about these tepid attempts at reform, did hiring practices actually change province by province? The most impactful reform was Ottawa's requirement that all university positions be advertised, open and competitive. There was no concerted effort to bring the talented pool of Canadian academics back to Canada from the U.S. who wanted to establish themselves in Canada again. There was no serious attempt to legislate that Canadian citizenship be an essential qualification for all new appointments, a central demand of Mathews and Steele.

Perhaps, the new requirement in the mid-70s that all jobs be advertised and hiring made more transparent was not the fundamental change that Mathews championed. Still, it effectively dismantled the informal old boy's network that had given many Americans tenured positions with a little more than a phone call. As a result, the proportion of Canadian-trained faculty improved substantially, but hiring Canadians with excellence as a priority of public policy hardly was resolved.

The Canada First Hiring Policy

There were high hopes for the Canada First hiring guidelines introduced by the Trudeau government in 1982 to ensure that Canadians were not discriminated against in the university hiring process. On close inspection, the Canada First hiring guidelines were more of an aspirational statement of soft law rather than the launch of a forceful new policy. There was no penalty for noncompliance. There was no oversight by provincial and federal governments. Faculty unions could not bring a grievance when the principles and practices were not followed as non-Canadians continued to be hired instead of homegrown candidates of excellence.

Even the name Canada First was misleading, creating the false impression that the hiring playing field had finally been levelled for qualified Canadian academics. That said, we can see now the tangible impact of Mathews' campaign. At many universities, hiring committees were required by their university to actively seek out qualified Canadians. It created a legal obligation to look for qualified Canadian candidates when creating a short list of prospective candidates. Recently PhDs trained in Canada were hired in increasing

---

[17]   Abraham Rothstein, "Binding Prometheus", in Ian Lumsden, op. cit., p.210.

numbers when positions were advertised even though there were fewer tenure track positions available. With the underfunding of the Universities, there were fewer new positions and with the abolition of compulsory retirement, Canadian academics were teaching longer and postponing retirement. Canadian graduate students with PhDs still faced limited career opportunities in academia because of the diminishing number of full-time, tenure-stream positions.

Despite this mismatch between recent PhD graduates and their career prospects, not all university hiring committees, deans and senior administrators followed the letter and spirit of the new guidelines. Nonetheless, for hiring committees, the Canada First hiring guidelines appeared on all university websites where jobs are advertised. It says boldly, "Canadians and permanent residents will be given priority". For most universities, Canadian-trained PhDs increasingly were hired by the 1980s and formal hiring practices no longer permitted a professor in Toronto to phone a friend in Boston with a job offer. With all this incremental change, should Robin Mathews take a victory lap?

According to Stephen High, the President of the Canadian Historical Association, current practice differs from university to university. In their report, the Association asks, is it time to restore the "Canadians First" hiring guidelines for Canadian universities?[18] To make matters infinitely more complicated, every university gives different instructions to faculty hiring committees and interprets this vague wording depending on their reading of the law. High said, "In practice, however, what does it mean to be "qualified"? Does it include anyone who is a strong candidate...Or does it signify the best candidate available in the international pool of applicants? Nor is there any more clarity in what is meant by giving Canadians "priority".[19]

Piecemeal Reform Doesn't Cut It

University reforms enacted by different federal and provincial governments were frequently low-level, and sometimes effective despite their very modest ambition. On the goal of employment equity, for instance, Employment and

---

[18] Stephen High, Pres. the Canadian historical Association, Report, Is It Time To Restore The Canadians First Hiring Guidelines For Canadian Universities?, CHA, Ottawa. https://cha-shc.ca/precarity/is-it-time-to-restore-the-canadians-first-hiring-guidelines-for-canadian-universities/

[19] CHR *Report on Precarity*, Stephen High, Prof. of History, Concordia University and President of The Canadian Historical Association May 2021.

Social Development Canada weakened the Canada First Program further by creating a very long list of exemptions for hiring committees and university senior administrators. "Academic consultants, graduate students, postdoctoral fellows, research award recipients, guest lecturers" and, most significantly, "citizens of the U.S. and Mexico appointed as professors at the University, College and seminary levels of the NAFTA" are exempt from its provisions".[20] The NAFTA Agreement and other changes subsequently enabled Americans to be shortlisted, directly competing against Canadians.[21]

A decade earlier when Ottawa cancelled special tax provisions, (it had been an additional incentive for Americans to come to Canada), according to Kim Nossal, a prominent International Relations professor, many ex-pats quickly returned to the United States.[22] Many had used their appointments to leverage better jobs in U.S. universities. With their exodus, more Canadians were hired to teach international relations and the citizenship composition improved enough that Nossal concluded American scholars no longer dominated the IR job market. With all these reform initiatives, the fortunes of the Canadianization movement ebbed and flowed, gradually losing its drive and potency. By the new century, it was a shadow of its former self.

In the absence of a coherent "Canadians First" federal policy, a core group of Canada's elite universities including the University of Toronto, McGill and UBC began hiring foreign professors in large numbers after 2007. Lachapelle and Yang write insightfully about the great reversal and divergence between this elite group and the rest of Canada's regional universities. Their evidence-based research found that "between 2007 and 2017 witnessed an all-time high of incoming U.S. PhD talents and an all-time low of Canadian recruits. For instance, McGill's Anthropology, Economics, and Political Science departments hired no Canadian PhDs during this period —as if there were no outstanding home-grown candidates."[23]

These 'reactionary' trends had occurred in the past and now returned stronger than ever, driven by the new buzzwords of "excellence", "globalization",

---

[20]   Employment Equity Resources, *Hiring Foreign Academics In Canada*, Employment And Social Development Canada, Hire A Temporary Foreign Worker With The Labour Market Impact Assessment, Ottawa, Government of Canada, February, 2023.

[21]   Ibid.

[22]   Nossal, op.cit.

[23]   Francois Lachapelle, Alvin X. Yang, "Decoding the Great Divergence in Canadian Academia - A Longitudinal Look at U12 Professorial Hiring" CAUT, *University Affairs*, forthcoming.

and "internationalization". At three of Canada's elite universities, the new rhetoric stressed international U.S. university rankings, competition in the global higher education EU/U.S. market and status and prestige in the Anglosphere. Effectively, once again, qualified Canadians were not considered for top university positions. Without strong leadership from Ottawa, many of Canada's deans and presidents increasingly chose the international job seeker over the Canadian one. It is no small irony that the Federal Department of Employment Equity led the charge promoting the new neoliberal market discourse even as it undermined the original, very modest Canada First guidelines.

Mathews and The Great Awakening

So, what is Robin's legacy as a nationalist, educator, whistleblower and public intellectual?[24]

Mathews' legacy provides us with a way to see beyond the hollow claim that excellence came through competitiveness and access to the American market. Certainly, it doesn't pass public scrutiny. The real stars of Canadian academe have always been local talent, like Charles Taylor, Sylvia Ostry, Janice Stein, Kari Levitt, Will Coleman, Will Kymlicka, Abe Rotstein, Naomi Klein and Mel Watkins, to name just a few. The idea that a degree from an East Coast American university is innately superior to Canadian training, and that context doesn't matter in a globalized age any longer is baseless. Where is the evidence?

This much we know. In recruiting full-time faculty, the question of native-born versus foreign-born and the importance of the postgraduate degree is too important to ignore. Cultural literacy is always rooted spatially in our public lives, practices and values. Mathews' big idea was that Canadian hiring practices are critical components for building a vibrant, university system of high significance and excellence.[25]

---

[24] For a conflicting assessment of the Canadianization movement post 2000, see Yves Gingras, "The end of the Canadianizing movement", CAUT, University affairs, November 8, 2010. He argues that globalization and international competition "have become the new God for which all universities must bow" and that Canadian universities are hiring fewer Canadian citizens, scholars and scholars with foreign PhDs.

[25] It is worth repeating, Canada has always welcomed foreign professors. It should come as no surprise to recall that the most distinguished and accomplished frequently American stars do not remain in Canada. For instance, Charles Tilly, Katherine McKinnon, Emmanuel

11

To situate Mathews in his time is to recognize that he was not some kind of lone ninja warrior, but a crucial instigator in the short-lived nationalist awakening in English Canada. The signing of NAFTA effectively shut down the nationalist option in English Canada to Canadianize its institutions. NAFTA gave American professors the right to be on a shortlist for hiring new faculty. That said, Mathews' most important achievement was to turn the spotlight on the crisis in Canada's universities and their urgent need for a new mandate. In ways he could not have anticipated, during the next two decades, these centres of knowledge, research and education would be transformed and modernized.

They would become the go-to places for aspiring writers, musicians, filmmakers, athletes, scientists, researchers, tech geniuses and urban-based grassroots political movements of every description. Rotstein's gloomy prediction that Canadians could never understand Americanization, let alone effectively resist it, was at best a half-truth. The campaign to Canadianize the university remains a watershed event in higher education.

We can see Mathew's fingerprints on the Symons Report, ending tax breaks for foreign professors, mandating all jobs be advertised and competitive, the Canada First Policy, and the adoption of equity goals for hiring women, First Nations and marginalized groups. By the beginning of the new century, Canadian studies had been transformed and were no longer ghettoized in one program or department without resources and research materials.

By 2023, Canadian university courses covered an enormous range of literacy and research. A sampling would include a focus on gender, First Nations, the environment, immigrant communities, Canadian literature, multiculturalism, LGBTQ+ rights, poverty, national narratives, domestic violence, post-colonialism, postmodernity, the transnational nation-state, culture and communication as well as class and inequality, to name but a few.

Nor is it surprising that Canadian universities have proved their critics wrong by becoming more diverse, Canadianized, global and pluralistic. In the early part of the century, the modern university positioned itself at the busy intersection of the labour market for professional training, accessibility

---

Wallerstein, each a distinguished scholar, accepted positions briefly in several of Canada's leading universities but stayed only a few years. They left to return to the United States to invest their time and energy in leadership roles in the American system of research and higher education. The exception that proves the rule is Marshall McLuhan, arguably one of Canada's global academic stars, who immigrated from the United States early in his career and spent his entire working life at the University of Toronto.

for mass education and upward mobility for middle-class Canadians. Post-NAFTA, the institutional dynamics of the universities lurched predictably toward a hard conservative direction, visibly transactional, competitive, corporatized and market-oriented.

The country always needs waypoints to guide us through this maze of Mathews' activism, disappointments and accomplishments. We can see now that Mathews' Canadianization campaign was from the start not a wilderness of single instances. He made a lasting contribution because his social and political activism resonated with the times. He impacted Canada's university culture to a degree that might surprise even him.

In Canada's bureaucratized, underfunded educational system, there never was a realistic possibility for the deep structural reform of Canada's universities that Mathews championed. Certainly, he couldn't do it on his own unless there was a matching national strategy led by Ottawa with buy-in from Canada's ten provinces. That possibility never existed under the Liberal governments nor under Harper's Conservatives. Still, he politicized the Canadianization movement and led it as far as his activism was impactful. Robin's campaign was remarkably far-reaching and influential; it had its own vital energy and a dynamic that set the Canadianization movement distinctively apart from other nationalist movements of the time.

Works Cited

Brym, Robert. "Our First 50 Years: A Note on the University of Toronto's Department of Sociology." *The Canadian Journal of Sociology / Cahiers canadiens de sociologie*, vol. 51, no. 3, 2014.

Cormier, Jeffrey. *The Canadianization Movement: Emergence, Survival and Success.* University of Toronto Press, 2004.

Employment And Social Development Canada. "Employment Equity Resources, Hiring Foreign Academics In Canada, Hire A Temporary Foreign Worker With The Labour Market Impact Assessment." Ottawa, Government of Canada, February 2023.

Gingras, Yves. "The end of the Canadianizing movement." CAUT, University Affairs, November 8, 2010.

Godfrey, Dave. *From Gordon to Watkins to You: The Battle For Control Of Our Economy.* New Press, 1970.

Gordon, Walter. *Storm Signals New Economic Policies For Canada.* McClelland and Stewart, 1975.

Grayson, Paul. "Struggles About Canadianization In Anthropology and Sociology." CAUT, December 2005.

High, Stephen. "Pres. the Canadian Historical Association, Report, *Is It Time To Restore The Canadians First Hiring Guidelines For Canadian Universities?*" CHA, Ottawa. https://cha-shc.ca/precarity/is-it-time-to-restore-the-canadians-first-hiring-guidelines-for-canadian-universities/

Innis, Harold. "Staples, Markets, And Cultural Change." *Selected Essays* edited by Daniel Drache, McGill Queens, 1993.

Lachapelle, Francois, and Alvin X. Yang. "Decoding the Great Divergence in Canadian Academia - A Longitudinal Look at U12 Professorial Hiring." CAUT, University Affairs.

Lee, Dennis. "Cadence, Country, Silence: Writing In Colonial Space." *Boundary 2*, vol. 3, no. 1, Autumn 1974, pp. 151-168.

Levitt, Kari. *Silent Surrender. The Multinational Corporation In Canada.* MacMillan, 1970.

Lumsden, Ian (editor). *Close The 49th Parallel ETC: The Americanization Of Canada.* University of Toronto Press, 1970.

Mathews, Robin, and James Steele (editors). *The Struggle For Canadian Universities: A Dossier.* New Press, 1969.

Nossal, Kim. "Homegrown IR: the Canadianization of International Relations." *Journal of Canadian Studies*, vol. 35, no. 1, Spring 2000.

Palmer, Bryan D. *Canada 1960s The Irony Of Identities In The Rebellious Era.* University of Toronto Press, 2009.

Porter, John. *The Vertical Mosaic, An Analysis Of Social Class In Canada.* University of Toronto Press, 1965.

Rothstein, Abraham. "Binding Prometheus." In Ian Lumsden (editor), p. 210.

Steele, James, and Robin Mathews. "Canadianization Revisited: A Comment on Cormier's 'The Canadianization Movement in Context'." *The Canadian Journal of Sociology / Cahiers canadiens de sociologie*, vol. 31, no. 4, Autumn 2006, pp. 491-508.

Symons, T.H.B. "To Know Ourselves, Report Of The Commission On Canadian Studies." AUCC, 1976.

"CHR Report on Precarity." Stephen High, Prof. of History, Concordia University and President of The Canadian Historical Association, May 2021.

ROBIN MATHEWS: AN APPRECIATION

By Duncan Cameron

R obin Mathews' profound influence on my thinking and professional work has inspired me to revisit his fundamental beliefs, his uphill public policy struggles and achievements, and the forces that shaped his left-nationalist advocacy to protect Canada's cultural and political autonomy.

As a student studying English literature with Robin at the University of Alberta, I experienced what exceptional teaching was all about: his example gave me an ideal to strive for in my own career. Over the years, his engagement with the community influenced my own activism, research and debate of issues of national interest. Later as the editor of *The Canadian Forum* magazine, Robin was an unseen presence at our editorial meetings, as the board decided what books to review, what stories and poetry to present and which political and economic events we covered in depth. Mathews' commitment to Canadian intellectual life inspired *The Forum's* editorial board during my decade-long sojourn as editor as we put together the magazine ten times each year.

The Only Place to Be

At the University of Alberta in the 1960s, Saturday classes were usually poorly attended. The exception was in English 210, an introductory course taught by Robin Mathews from 1963 to 1964. What I discovered at 8:30 a.m. on Saturday mornings is what makes a lecture special. There was no other place I wanted to be when he was at the front of the class, sharing his love of literature. Even the Engineering and Commerce students, who were taking this obligatory course, were present regularly.

As a lecturer, Robin made poetry comprehensible and illuminating by turning complex text into meaningful stories and ideas. I recall how he moved seamlessly from *King Lear*[1] to local author W.O. Mitchell's novel *Who Has Seen the Wind*,[2] interpreting Shakespeare's genius while exploring

---

[1]   Shakespeare, William. *King Lear*. Oxford: Clarendon Press, 1877.
[2]   Mitchell, W.O. *Who Has Seen The Wind*. Toronto: Macmillan of Canada, 1947.

Mitchell's writing about a boy's life on the Canadian prairies. Some sixty years later, I still remember how Mathews' reading of T.S. Eliot's "The Wasteland"[3] invited this early morning class to consider the complexity of twentieth-century ideas, before bringing us to appreciate Ferlinghetti's collection, A Coney Island of the Mind,[4] with its portrayal of post-World War II American alienation.

At the first lecture, Robin explained that he was always available in his office to discuss literature, adding that he did not want students to stop by simply to invite him for a beer at the Macdonald Hotel. "If I want to have a beer, I will call my friends and go out with them," he said, "and you can do the same with your friends." In a vast, impersonal university, having a professor maintain an open door to discuss course material with undergraduates was uncommon. Still, it was Robin's way of living the student-professor relationship, and it was during English 210 that I began my enduring and meaningful friendship with him.

Left Nationalist Consciousness and the Canadian University

In 1970, I attended a packed gymnasium at UBC to hear Robin speak about his campaign on behalf of the "Canadianization of the Canadian University." In 1969, he co-authored, with his Carleton English Department colleague James Steele, The Struggle for Canadian Universities.[5] Their study stands as a landmark of the left nationalist movement, not least because it was a campaign that became a major success. Most did not. Mathews' work helped to ignite the growth of Canadian consciousness among Anglophones during the late 1960s. This new awareness was particularly evident in the arts and culture sector, where Canadian novels, theatre, visual arts, and popular music found expanding audiences. In Quebec, the Quiet Revolution provided a rousing example of what could be achieved for those, like Mathews, who were paying attention to the mood of the country. He was a different kind of academic, and his influence paved the way for me to become an academic activist, opposing free trade with the U.S., exposing the campaign promoting deficit and debt reduction and objecting to Prime Minister Brian Mulroney's constitutional agenda.

---

[3] Eliot, T. S. The Waste Land: and Other Poems, 1888-1965. London: Faber and Faber, 1999.
[4] Ferlinghetti, Lawrence. A Coney Island of the Mind: Poems. New York: New Directions Books, 1958.
[5] Mathews, Robin and Steele, James Arthur. The Struggle for Canadian Universities: A Dossier. Toronto: New Press, 1969.

Universities provided a fertile ground for left nationalism. The Mathews and Steele campaign inspired the Federal government to instigate legislation directing universities to give priority to Canadians applying for post-secondary teaching jobs.[6] Many applicants of my age found university teaching positions because of this legislation, even though it did not bind universities to its provisions, nor could it have done so while preserving university autonomy. Nevertheless, there was a crying need for change in hiring practices at our universities. In her book, *Long Way from Home*,[7] Myrna Kostash points out that the faculty at the University of Alberta's Department of Sociology was made up of members from the U.S. Pacific Northwest.[8] The Department of Political Science offered no courses on Canadian provincial politics, Alberta politics, or the city politics of Edmonton. At the time, a visiting professor from London, Ontario, taught the one Canadian political science course.

U.S. Imperialism and Canada

When I returned to Canada in 1975, after completing my doctoral studies in France, and joining the Political Science Department at the University of Ottawa, my parents moved from Edmonton to Vancouver. On visits home, one of my pleasures was to meet with Robin. In 1984, he and his wife Esther left Ottawa to relocate to Vancouver. Usually, I would arrive at his home near Commercial Drive after dinner. We would drink coffee and talk. The conversation often lasted very late, and on more than one occasion, I left after four o'clock in the morning. Mainly, we discussed our shared concerns about the hazardous effects of American imperialism on Canada. Mathews had alerted the country to what was going on with the Americanization of the university, and I had discovered, as a junior officer in the Department of Finance in Ottawa, the enormous financial implications of the control of Canadian industry by U.S. companies. The problem of the supremacy of the U.S. dollar in world finance and what to do about it motivated my doctoral research after I left the Finance Department.

---

[6] High, Steven. "There is No Solidarity in a Meritocracy: Precarity in the History Profession in Canada". A Report by Steven High, Vice-President, Canadian Historical Association, ActiveHistory.ca, 13 May 2021.

[7] Kostash, Myrna. *Long Way from Home: The Story of the Sixties Generation in Canada*. Toronto: J. Lorimer, 1980.

[8] Cormier, Jeffery. *The Canadianization Movement: Emergence, Survival, and Success*. Toronto: University of Toronto Press, 2004, 65.

In 1944, as World War II was ending, the Bretton Woods Conference established the U.S. dollar at the center of international finance. Instead of having nations settle payment deficits directly through cooperation among central banks, as the British Keynes Plan proposed, Wall St. bankers succeeded in establishing foreign exchange markets as the principal mechanism for settling debts. The foreign exchange market provided lucrative fees to banks. It has become the largest of all world markets. Currencies are traded in pairs; each national currency is traded against the U.S. dollar. As a result, all nations need to acquire dollars to hold as central bank reserves to settle debts with other countries, making the U.S. dollar the world reserve currency. This use by the world of the U.S. dollar as the means of payment internationally gave the U.S. what was identified as an "exorbitant privilege": the ability to buy abroad using its currency, while other countries had first to acquire dollars before purchasing abroad. As the U.S. spent abroad, nations built up their holdings of U.S. dollars. The dollars held abroad were the equivalent of a credit loan allotted to the U.S. to do as it pleased because the holder had no intention of redeeming the dollars being held as reserves. What the Americans were doing with that ever-expanding loan was buying up companies abroad.

The passive attitude of Canadian governments to U.S. corporate takeovers of Canadian industry provoked a strong reaction from left nationalists; among them was Robin Mathews. It was the Canadian central banker James Coyne who, in the 1960s, first sounded the alarm about U.S. investment in Canada. Liberal Walter Gordon, in a Royal Commission report,[9] a book[10] and lectures, explained how U.S. control over Canadian industry was increasing American influence in Canadian politics. The book that best captured the spirit of the left nationalists was *Silent Surrender* by Kari Levitt.[11] She explained how outflows to the U.S. from Canada of interest, dividends, and profits exceeded inflows of U.S. ownership and investment capital. This contradicted with statistics the idea that Canada was a net financial beneficiary from U.S. investment. In fact, U.S. multinationals invested abroad because they reaped large profits as a result.

As Finance Minister, in his 1963 budget, Gordon introduced measures to limit the flow of new American investment. The very American forces in

---

[9] Gordon, Walter L. *Royal Commission on Canada's Economic Prospects, Final Report*. Ottawa: Canada Privy Council, 1958.

[10] Gordon, Walter L. *A Choice for Canada*. Toronto: McClelland and Stewart Ltd., 1966.

[11] Levitt, Kari. *Silent Surrender*. Toronto: The Macmillan Company of Canada Limited, 1970.

Canada he pointed to as overly powerful were able to thwart his action, and the budget measures were withdrawn. Gordon resigned from Prime Minister Lester B. Pearson's federal cabinet after the 1965 election but returned to Cabinet in 1967 after Lester Pearson promised to create a Taskforce on Foreign Ownership, the Watkins Commission.[12]

The issue of foreign ownership became central to the left-nationalist movement that was gathering strength in various sectors of Canadian society. As an activist, Robin Mathews became vocal on issues that went beyond the struggle he led in the university sector. Major public opinion battles were waging over Canadian complicity in the U.S.–Vietnam War, looming ecological crises, the plight of poor countries, and prospects for international economic development. The new Canadian consciousness expressed by left-nationalists asserted its mark on a generation and the country. The left-nationalists were prominent dissenters on specific issues such as the Mulroney free trade deal. In sectors where Canadians were struggling to overcome American predominance, including publishing, cinema, radio and television broadcasting, nationalists received some public support. *The Perilous Trade*, published in 2003 by Roy MacSkimming,[13] though a book about book publishing, provides a history of Canadian cultural policy and left nationalism.

A Communitarian Canadian

In *Life and Times of Liberal Democracy*, C.B. Macpherson[14] discussed how the transition to an authentic democracy was constrained by the predominance of property rights over civic rights. In effect, individual property rights trumped community concerns. In the U.S., the traditions of rugged individualism, liberty and the pursuit of happiness were linked to the accumulation of wealth and property. For Bertrand Russell, whose writings were much admired by Robin, American individualism led to a sort of anarchism, a society of one

---

[12]   Watkins, Mel. "Task Force on Foreign Ownership and the Structure of Canadian Investment". *The Canadian Encyclopedia*, Historica Canada, 16 December 2013. Despite having been commissioned by the Privy Council there is no official reference available to its publication.

[13]   MacSkimming,Roy. *The Perilous Trade: Publishing Canada's Writers*. Toronto: McClelland and Stewart, 2003.

[14]   Macpherson,C.B. *The Life and Times of Liberal Democracy*. Oxford: Oxford University Press, 1977.

against all. For Robin, such conflict was antithetical to the communitarian nature of Canada.[15]

In adopting the Canadian Charter of Rights and Freedoms, despite serious objections from big business and their spokespeople in parliament, property rights were excluded, in effect confirming the priority of liberal civic rights in Canada. While entrenching the protection of minority rights, and particularly the equality rights of women, unlike the U.N. Declaration of Human Rights, the Charter fell short of protecting economic and social rights. For left-nationalist critics, these exemptions kept the door open to austerity policies that made life more precarious, weakened the social fabric and increased social inequalities. In fact, for much of the last fifty years, Canadian public policy has favoured the accumulation of wealth by already wealthy individuals—as if this would somehow reduce poverty.

The model of liberal democracy C.B. Macpherson attributed to Canada and other industrialized nations was limited to electoral democracy: democracy primarily voting in elections. Voters were consumers choosing a product in the marketplace. Moreover, like average consumers, voters were influenced by image, packaging, advertising, and marketing. In the age introduced by television, the party leader was the product people looked at, with the party an important factor, yet secondary.

Robin's concerns with the direction of Canadian public life would lead him to establish a political party to contest federal elections. The National Party was founded in 1979. It was alive in both the 1979 and 1980 elections, with Robin a losing candidate in Ottawa Centre both times. Given his experience founding a political party, Robin was also sympathetic to the efforts of Mel Hurtig to launch his version of the National Party to contest the 1993 election. While Hurtig finished ahead of the incumbent M.P., he still finished third in Edmonton Northwest.

Robin and I only spoke rarely about party politics, with our conversations turning toward the national policy issues that interested us both. I remember him being pleased that the Liberal Party had been defeated in 1984. However, we agreed that with Brian Mulroney as Prime Minister, Canadians had elected the most anti-national government in its history. It turned out to be the case with Mulroney's Conservative government. By signing the North American Free Trade Agreement (NAFTA) in 1992, the Mulroney government signed

---

[15] Mathews, Robin. *Canadian Identity: Major Forces Shaping the Life of a People.* Ottawa: Steel Rail Publishing, 1988.

away some of the powers the Canadian Parliament and Provincial Legislatures needed to govern and agreed that Canada would align itself to cooperate with the U.S. on foreign policy issues. You could not have designed a better device for limiting Canadian sovereignty and democratic practices than NAFTA.

Before the Free Trade Agreement, during the left-nationalist period of the 1960s and 1970s government included measures to promote airplay for Canadian music, limit the tax advantages of American periodicals in the Canadian marketplace, extend support to Canadian publishers and authors, as well as support the Mathews-Steele legislation directing universities to advertise job vacancies, give priority to Canadian candidates, and only hire foreigners when it could be demonstrated there were no eligible Canadian candidates.

Despite these measures, popular culture in English-speaking Canada remained predominantly American. With the Free Trade Agreement, the opportunities for Canadian artists and writers to access their market were further limited by the cultural provisions of NAFTA. While the trade deal acknowledged the legitimacy of Canadian measures to promote domestic cultural industries (note the American use of "industries" to describe the Arts), it also granted the Americans the right to respond to any such measures by opposing measures of equivalent effect directed at any sector of the Canadian economy. In effect, no Canadian government was going to test that provision of the agreement. The so-called cultural exemption was toothless. American cultural imperialism rested easy.

An Unseen Presence

In 1989, when my book publisher, James Lorimer, became the owner and publisher of *The Canadian Forum*, he invited me to become the editor. The magazine would relocate from Toronto to Ottawa, and my first task was assembling an editorial board. In *The Ottawa Citizen*, Robin reviewed *Willie: A Romance*,[16] a novel by Heather Robertson, a writer I greatly admired. In her preface, she thanked Roy MacSkimming for his editorial assistance. I called Roy, introduced myself, and asked if we could meet. He agreed to join the editorial board. It turned out he had published the Mathews and Steele book *The Struggle for Canadian Universities* when he and Dave Godfrey founded

---

[16]   Robertson, Heather. *Willie: A Romance*. Toronto: James Lorimer & Company Ltd., Publishers, 1983.

New Press in 1969-70. *The Struggle for Canadian Universities* was the inaugural publication of this storied publishing house.

In short order, I recruited an editorial board with strong ties to Robin. I held Pat Smart of Carleton University in the highest regard. In my view, there was no more brilliant academic of my generation than Pat, who had become a close colleague and friend of Robin's when they were both teaching at Carleton. Tracy Morey, formerly of the CBC and then a Communications officer with CUPE, was well known to me. She had been a neighbour and friend of Robin's. Our managing editor, John Urquhart, was a former student of Robin's at Carleton. Later, Penny Sanger, another friend and former neighbour of Robin's, would join the board.

Robin was an unseen presence at our editorial meetings. Roy explained at our first meeting that *The Forum* should pay writers, even if it is a small amount. Paying writers was a departure from the practice since the magazine's inception in 1920 when it was agreed that ego income would suffice for remuneration.

Remunerating writers was a sure way to promote writing as a profession in Canada. Without a cadre of professional writers with access to outlets for their work, Canadian readers would inevitably be left with a choice of American or British magazines and books to read. Canadian life could only diminish in importance as a result.

Countries like Britain and the U.S. had developed a language for discussing national issues largely through fostering publications such as *The New Statesman* or *The New Republic*. The role of *The Canadian Forum* was to encourage Canadians to generate their own shared language to discuss their issues and, in the process, grow the national conversation.

Before I had convened the first editorial meeting, I met with Robin in Vancouver to discuss my new undertaking: editing *The Forum*. His first consideration was to ensure that poetry occupied its traditional place of honour. Margaret Atwood's very first publication was a poem in *The Forum*,[17] where Northrop Frye, her mentor, had once been the editor.

In the wake of the Free Trade Agreement, Robin and I agreed that we were going to see the departure of many American multinationals as they shut down Canadian operations and relocated back to their homeland. Pointing to economic tools governments could use in the new environment was going to be an editorial preoccupation of the magazine.

---

[17]   Atwood, M.E. "about peonies...and more". *The Canadian Forum*, 1960.

Robin believed that you could not draw a line between politics and culture and that the two fit together. For our editorial coverage, that meant treating cultural policies as important as political issues for understanding and bolstering Canadian democracy and sovereignty. Publishing a story by Darryl Duke about the need for President Patrick Watson to redo the CBC was as important as doing a root-and-branch critique of the Governor of the Bank of Canada's high-interest rate policies. In the early 1990s, I invited Robin to attend an editorial meeting on one of his rare visits to Ottawa. Uncharacteristically, he seemed to prefer enjoying the conversation without feeling the need to take a leading, critical role. It was as if he felt very much at home in the company of long-time friends who shared his passion for things Canadian.

Championing Canadian Thought

When I was well into academic life at the University of Ottawa, Robin called. He wanted me to connect with Leslie Armour, a colleague in the Philosophy Department at Ottawa U. Leslie was a towering intellect with wide interests, but as a champion of Canadian writing and teaching, he was facing opposition to his work. In 1981, Armour had just co-authored with Elizabeth Trott, *The Faces of Reason: An Essay on Philosophy and Culture in English Canada 1850-1950*,[18] a major work that promised to have a long shelf life. When Leslie proposed to teach a course on Canadian philosophy, his department committee was against the idea, and Armour's appeal to the Dean of Arts was rejected. How could there be a "Canadian" philosophy, his colleagues asked? Leslie provided an answer. Everything has a geography and a history, and that includes schools of philosophical thought. Armour continued developing his ideas despite the lack of understanding of his work within his Department and Faculty. Anxious to make this thinking about Canadian philosophy available to a broader audience, in 1981, Leslie published *The Idea of Canada and the Crisis of Community*[19] with Robin and Esther's publishing company, Steel Rail Educational Publishing, which they operated from their dining room.

---

[18] Armour, Leslie and Trott, Elizabeth. *The Faces of Reason: An Essay on Philosophy and Culture in English Canada 1850–1950*. Waterloo, Ontario: Wilfrid Laurier University Press, 1981.

[19] Armour, Leslie. *The Idea of Canada and the Crisis of Community*. Ottawa: Steel Rail Publishing, 1981.

For Robin Mathews, culture was the foundation of an economy and the politics of a country. What he prized was Indigenous cultural creation. What repelled him was the impact of American popular culture consumed in Canada. Graham Spry, a founder of CBC Radio-Canada, famously said in advancing the project of public broadcasting in Canada: "The choice is between the state or the United States." Like Spry, Robin looked to the federal government to be conscious of its responsibility to incubate and sustain Canadian cultural undertakings.

In addition to fighting for the Canadianization of the university, launching the National Party, and with his wife, playing a central role in managing a publishing company, Robin was a founder of Ottawa's The Great Canadian Theatre Company. While his focus was on national issues and institution building, Robin was attentive to individual Canadian novelists, poets, and playwrights. He vigorously championed their works.

Protest and Justice

As an English professor at the University of Alberta in the mid-1960s, Robin made headlines in Edmonton when he stood up in the visitors' gallery at a City Council meeting and read a petition calling on Mayor William Hawrelak to resign. In 1959, an enquiry headed by Justice Porter into land dealings by the mayor had found Hawrelak guilty of gross misconduct for attempting on six occasions to rezone property he owned to his advantage. Hawrelak, who was first elected in 1951, then resigned as mayor and was sued by the city. Hawrelak settled the suit by paying $100,000 (plus costs) in fines.[20] In the highly contested 1963 election, marred by a mob attack on students protesting the re-election campaign of the disgraced mayor, Hawrelak was returned to office. For Robin, this amounted to an outrage to public decency. Hawrelak had made himself ineligible for office and should resign rather than take up his position again. This was the argument Mathews made in his address to the Council.

As a result of his public protest, Robin was singled out for disturbing the peace and causing public mischief. He was arrested and jailed. This event was the beginning of a saga. Robin planned to contest the charges and sought a lawyer to defend him in court. It turned out that it took four months before one of the city's litigators was willing to take his case.

---

[20] Stuemer, Diane King. 1992. *Hawrelak: The Story*. Calgary, Alberta: Script: the Writers Group Inc., 150.

At the time and by coincidence, I crossed paths with Robin on the snowy grounds between the University of Alberta's Rutherford Library and the Arts building. He was wearing his second-hand coat made of buffalo pelt, originally worn by an Edmonton police officer for whom these coats were standard issue. "How are you doing, Professor Mathews?" I asked. He replied that he was headed for the Law Library to speak to the Law Faculty students about their profession. I asked to tag along.

Mathews entered the reading room reserved for law students, climbed up on a table, giving him a good view of the room, and began an impromptu speech about justice, the law, and the legal profession. His message was that lawyers were supposed to serve the cause of justice, not simply do the bidding of those with the means to pay. No lawyer should be intimidated from serving justice by the powers that be in society—as was the entire legal profession in Edmonton.

Robin hardly expected a standing ovation and did not get one. The students reacted as if they had already joined the ranks of their chosen profession and were indifferent to calls for defending the public interest. Yet, I suspect at least one budding lawyer present was impressed by the uninvited orator. I was convinced that Robin exposed the legal profession for its lack of concern for the public interest by seeing justice pursued.

Throughout his adult life, Robin was an advocate for justice. That an academic would step into civil society on behalf of the common good— protecting public office from corruption—was an eye-opener for me. What was speaking out of turn for many was Robin's way of engaging with Canada and calling high profile people out. Making trouble for the powers that be, that was the Mathews creed. He lived it. I admired him for it. I always will.

Works Cited

Armour, Leslie. *The Idea of Canada and the Crisis of Community*. Ottawa: Steel RailPublishing,1981.

Armour, Leslie and Trott, Elizabeth. *The Faces of Reason: An Essay on Philosophy and Culture in English Canada 1850–1950*. Waterloo, Ontario:Wilfrid Laurier University Press, 1981.

Atwood, M.E. "about peonies...and more". *The Canadian Forum*, 1960.

Cormier, Jeffery. *The Canadianization Movement: Emergence, Survival, and Success*. Toronto: University of Toronto Press, 2004.

Eliot, T. S. *The Waste Land: and Other Poems*, 1888-1965. London: Faber and Faber, 1999.

Ferlinghetti, Lawrence. *A Coney Island of the Mind: Poems.* New York: New Directions Books, 1958.

Gordon, Walter L. *Royal Commission on Canada's Economic Prospects, Final Report.* Ottawa: Canada Privy Council, 1958,

Gordon, Walter L. *A Choice for Canada.* Toronto: McClelland and Stewart Ltd., 1966.

High, Steven. "There is No Solidarity in a Meritocracy: Precarity in the History Profession in Canada".A Report by Steven High, Vice-President, Canadian Historical Association, ActiveHistory.ca, 13 May 2021.

Kostash, Myrna. *Long Way from Home: The Story of the Sixties Generation in Canada.* Toronto: J. Lorimer, 1980.

Levitt, Kari. *Silent Surrender.* Toronto: The Macmillan Company of Canada Limited, 1970.

Macpherson,C.B. *The Life and Times of Liberal Democracy.* Oxford: Oxford University Press, 1977.

MacSkimming,Roy. *The Perilous Trade: Publishing Canada's Writers.* Toronto: McClelland and Stewart, 2003.

Mathews, Robin. *Canadian Identity: Major Forces Shaping the Life of a People.* Ottawa: Steel Rail Publishing, 1988.

Mathews, Robin and Steele, James Arthur. *The Struggle for Canadian Universities: A Dossier.*Toronto: New Press, 1969.

Mitchell, W.O. *Who Has Seen the Wind.* Toronto: Macmillan of Canada, 1947.

Robertson,Heather. *Willie: A Romance.* Toronto: James Lorimer & Company Ltd., Publishers, 1983.

Shakespeare, William. *King Lear.* Oxford: Clarendon Press, 1877.

Stuemer, Diane King. 1992. *Hawrelak: The Story.* Calgary, Alberta: Script: the Writers Group Inc.

Watkins, Mel. "Task Force on Foreign Ownership and the Structure of Canadian Investment". *The Canadian Encyclopedia*, Historica Canada, 16 December 2013.

WORKING WITH ROBIN MATHEWS ON THE TRANSFORMATION OF FRENCH DEPARTMENTS AND THE STRUGGLE FOR CANADIANIZATION AT CARLETON

By Sinclair Robinson, Pat Smart and Donald Smith

When Joyce Wayne approached us with a request that we write about the transformation of French Department course offerings brought about by a report we wrote in 1972 under Robin's guidance, we searched among our boxes of old documents and found a trove of material related not only to the "French Report" but to subsequent battles we waged with Robin for a heightened awareness of Canadian and French-Canadian issues at Carleton University and beyond. Already committed nationalists when we began to work with Robin, we subsequently threw ourselves into the breach along with him on any Canada-related issues that came up at Carleton in the next few years. This article will focus primarily on our Report on French Departments across the country but will also give examples of other issues with which we grappled, not only in Carleton University publications like the student newspaper *The Charlatan* and the faculty newsletter *This Week Times Two*, but in media interventions outside Carleton.

At Carleton University in the spring of 1972, when we first met with Robin Mathews to discuss writing what we would later call the "French report," Robin was a charismatic professor of Canadian literature in the English department, known for the important work *The Struggle for Canadian Universities* he had co-edited with his colleague Jim Steele in 1969. He was already a friend of Pat's from their work together in the Waffle movement in the NDP, which had produced a manifesto titled *For An Independent, Socialist Canada*. Donald remembers meeting him at a press conference where Robin stated, "Everything is political: the water we drink, the food we eat, the air we breathe and the survival of Canadian culture." As for us, we were all junior untenured members of the Department of French, then staffed by professors mainly of British or European background who had little if any knowledge of Canadian or Quebec literature and culture. Of thirty-eight faculty members, only five or six had Canadian backgrounds. As for the curriculum, it included just one course in French-Canadian literature, and language courses were exclusively devoted to "Parisian" French. An important member of our team was Robin's student, Joyce Wayne, who co-authored the Report.

As graduates of Honours French from Ontario universities, the three of us were painfully aware of the shortcomings of French departments. We knew that in our own case, becoming familiar with Quebec and French Canada was largely a do-it-yourself venture. In Canadian French departments, language and literature courses were taught the same way as in the UK or the U.S., often with the same materials, and the French language, as presented in these courses, was associated exclusively with France. Faculty members made little or no effort to include even passing references to Quebec or French Canada. By that omission, students were led to believe that a large part of the country's language, literature, and culture were not worth learning about. At the University of Toronto, where Pat had done her undergraduate studies, French-Canadian literature was introduced to students in a half course taught in the final term of the fourth year, in which, in the year Pat took the course, the professor began the course by informing the students that she was unfamiliar with all of the works on the course curriculum and that each student would therefore be responsible for presenting one of the authors studied. (As negative as this may sound, this forced specialization led Pat to her first publication[1], and her choice to continue her studies in French-Canadian literature at Laval University the following year.) At the University of Western Ontario, where Sinclair had done his undergraduate work, there was one course in French Canadian literature, but it was not available to Honours students, only those in the Pass BA. Sinclair immersed himself in Canadian French through an exchange visit with a Quebec family and a summer working in a restaurant in east-end Montreal. After his BA, he studied linguistics and specialized in the French language in Canada. Donald did his Honours BA at the newly founded bilingual Glendon College at York University. He spent his third year at Laval University in Quebec, thanks to an exchange between Glendon and Laval created by Professor Jacques Cotnam, a specialist in Quebec literature

---

[1] "The Agonizing Solitude: The Poetry of Anne Hébert", *Canadian Literature* 10 (Autumn 1961), 51-61. Reprinted in *Contemporary Literary Criticism* (ed. Jean C. Stine), Gale Research Company, 1980.

who was a major influence on Donald's later decision to specialize in the area. "The year was 1967", Donald recalls, "General De Gaulle was calling 'Vive le Québec libre' from the balcony of Montreal's City Hall, and the Parti Québécois was in the process of being created." All of us had familiarized ourselves with Quebec culture through interprovincial visits, summer jobs in Quebec, and graduate studies at Quebec universities or at the University of Ottawa.

Our Report (*French-Canadian Studies and Their Place in University French Departments. A Critique and a Model for Change in English Canada*) contained a survey of French Department offerings across the country based on a thorough examination of the calendars of each university and consultations with faculty members across the country. It listed the faculty members who supported our aims and provided information and insights as we put together our figures and subsequently signed the Report. The figures we amassed showed the stark reality: French-Canadian Studies were neglected across the country. An important and influential aspect of the Report was that, in addition to summarizing the results of this survey, we included a detailed, four-year model program specializing in French-Canadian literature, thought and language, complete with a detailed bibliography, which was impressive enough to convince even the general reader that the field of French-Canadian literary studies and linguistics was indeed rich and deserving of detailed study. The proposed program allowed for specialization in one of three areas: French literature and culture, French-Canadian literature and culture, or language and linguistics, with students required to take a minimum number of courses in each of these areas. This represented a radical departure from traditional programs, which, besides almost completely ignoring French-Canadian literature, gave short shrift to language and linguistics, not to mention the language and linguistics of Quebec French.

The Report was sent to all department chairs and student governments across the country as well as to the Commission on Canadian Studies[2] and to the media in September 1972, and it evoked an immediate reaction. There were newspaper articles, radio and TV interviews, and, as hoped, comments from French department members across the country. The Report was the subject

---

2   The Commission on Canadian Studies was established in 1972 by the Association of Universities and Colleges of Canada (AUCC). See https://archives.trentu.ca/index.php/86-031.

of articles in *Le Devoir*,[3] *La Presse*, and the Ottawa newspapers[4], and an article was distributed by Canadian Press. Donald remembers receiving a phone call from the influential Professor David Hayne of the French Department of the University of Toronto. Professor Hayne told him that the Report was creating ripples in his Department, but that he thought it was necessary and would continue discussing it with his colleagues. In our own Department, the shock was palpable. Not only had the Report been authored by untenured faculty members, but it also seemed as if all of Canada (if one judged by the media reports) agreed with them. Sinclair remembers how one colleague switched overnight from 'tu' to 'vous' when addressing him as a result of the Report. Pat believes that the fact that she was granted tenure two years later, in preference over a colleague from France, was not unrelated to the impact of the Report. In fact, we could say that the hiring of three Canadians (Robinson, Smith and Smart) in 1969, 1970 and 1971 was not unrelated to the work begun by Mathews and Steele in 1968. As was their eventual tenure.

Only Robin's inspiration and example could have led junior untenured faculty to take on the establishment as we did in the Report and after. In an interview in the *Ottawa Journal*, Donald Smith denounced a Carleton-sponsored study tour of France for conversational practice as "an Eiffel Tower approach"[5] that was an insult to French Canadians. The three of us, along with another colleague, signed a letter to *Le Droit* criticizing the CBC program *Pardon My French* for its refusal to endorse the French-Canadian pronunciation of many words[6]. And in the Carleton faculty newsletter *This Week*, Sinclair and Pat took up arms against Mordecai Richler, the writer in residence in the English department that year, who had stated in the prestigious Plaunt lectures of March 1973 that culture was about "excellence" and that by subsidizing Canadian art the government was "licencing mediocrity and twice-blessing the second rate." In response, Robinson pointed out that Britain, France and even the United States have measures in place to protect their cultural productions and hiring practices. Smart challenged Richler's argument that by subsidizing Canadian art, governments "licence mediocrity and twice-bless the second rate."

---

[3]   Un rapport de Carleton: Les universités anglophones ignorent l'apport culturel du Canada français. » *Le Devoir*, October 11, 1972, p. 18.

[4]   "University French courses get poor rating in study" *Ottawa Journal*, October 11, 1972, p. 27.

[5]   "Eiffel Tower study attacked", *Ottawa Journal*, April 12, 1975.

[6]   "*Pardon my French*": Letter to *Le Droit* April 24, 1972, p. 6.

On the contrary, she stated, Canadians are learning that "to be fully human means to be conscious and part of a community, that a play or a poem or a good novel can be not only an encounter with universal values, but a discovery of those values through the formalization of their own experience"[7]. During these same heady years, Robin was conducting his campaign for Canadianization on several fronts, including letters to Carleton deans and administrators, as well as constant interventions in Carleton publications and other media outlets. In 1974, he released a thirty-five-page report denouncing Carleton's hiring practices as "racist", citing eleven academic positions that were not advertised, or advertised late, in Canadian publications, of which eight were filled by non-Canadians.[8]

These were heady years, charged with the excitement of discovering and defending our culture and the culture of Quebec, always inspired and accompanied by Robin, who seemed indefatigable. Our first academic publications built on the content and intent of the Report, with Donald and Sinclair co-authoring in 1973 a best-selling *Handbook of Canadian French*[9] designed to introduce to the English Canadian public, in a practical way, the particularities of the French language in Canada. This was the first publication of its kind. In the same vein, in 1974. Smith and Robinson published a classroom edition of Claude Jasmin's joual novel *Pleure pas, Germaine* [10], with the aim of developing in language students an appreciation of that aspect of the language, another first in English Canada. Smart's 1973 *Hubert Aquin agent double*[11] was the first study published on Quebec novelist Hubert Aquin. But did any of it have a lasting effect?

Gradually, over the next decade or two, many departments moved toward giving greater space to French-Canadian studies. The old course divisions based on the various centuries of French literature gave way to more thematic and contemporary approaches, often requiring a minimum of courses with French Canadian content. Language and linguistics also acquired new importance. In our own Department at Carleton, within two or three years, the program was transformed to better reflect the rightful place of French-

---

[7]   *Forum: Richler under Fire, This Week Times Two*, April 3, 1973, vol. 5, no. 22.

[8]   *Racism at Carleton University: a study and report*, 1976, 35 pages.

[9]   *Practical Handbook of Canadian French*. Toronto: Macmillan of Canada, 1973. 172 pp.

[10]   *Pleure pas, Germaine* by Claude Jasmin. Montreal: Centre éducatif et culturel, 1974. 159 pp. Edition for English-speaking students with introduction, notes, questions and vocabulary.

[11]   *Hubert Aquin, agent double; la dialectique de l'art et du pays dans "Prochain épisode" et "Trou de mémoire"*, Montréal :Presses de l'Université de Montréal, 1973.

Canadian studies, and parallel specializations in literature and in language/ linguistics were instituted.

The French Report, then, played a crucial part in the evolution of French departments across the country. Of course, the ideal represented in the Report has rarely, if ever, been achieved, but the continuous evolution of offerings demonstrates the openness and renewal that the Report advocated. Thanks to student demand, French literature has become the poorer cousin of Quebec and *la francophonie*, and more and more French language courses take into account the different varieties of French in the world and, in the case of Canada, Canadian French. Most recently, French departments, like all other Humanities departments, have been under threat of being diminished and even disappearing as demands and funding priorities shift to more "job-oriented" areas. But the efforts to broaden and improve the place of Quebec and French Canada in French department curricula continue and must continue. Just as in so many other endeavours, English Canada must constantly resist the idea that content from abroad should supersede our own, that what happens here is somehow less important than what happens elsewhere. We should not be denied the opportunity to learn about what affects us directly, in our own country. In all these things, Robin Mathews was an indefatigable mentor, missionary and gadfly who transformed the consciousness and commitment of all three of us as well as helping to move Canadian culture in directions that validated both English and French-speaking Canada.

Works Cited

Jasmin, Claude. *Pleure pas, Germaine*. Montreal: Centre éducatif et culturel, 1974. 159 pp. Edition for English-speaking students with introduction, notes, questions and vocabulary by Sinclair Robinson and Donald Smith.

Mathews, Robin, *Racism at Carleton University: a study and report*, 1976.

Mathews, Robin et al. *French-Canadian Studies and Their Place in University French Departments. A Critique and a Model for Change in English Canada*, 1972 (published by the authors).

Mathews, Robin and J.S. Steele, eds. *The Struggle for Canadian Universities*. Toronto, New Press, 1969.

Purcell, Patricia. "The Agonizing Solitude: The Poetry of Anne Hébert," *Canadian Literature* 10 (Autumn 1961), pp. 51-61. Reprinted in *Contemporary Literary Criticism* (Jean C. Stine. ed.), Gale Research Company, 1980.

Robinson, Sinclair and Smith, Donald. *Practical Handbook of Canadian French*. Toronto: Macmillan of Canada, 1973,172 pp.

Smart, Patricia. *Hubert Aquin, agent double; la dialectique de l'art et du pays dans "Prochain épisode" et "Trou de mémoire"*, Montréal: Les Presses de l'Université de Montréal (Coll. « Lignes québécoises »), 1973, 138 pp.

ROBIN MATHEWS AND THE CANADIANIZATION OF TRADE UNIONS

By Alvin Finkel

In November 1969, Robin Mathews wrote to McGill University economist Kari Levitt, whose painstaking research on the extent of American control of the Canadian economy would soon thereafter be published in *Silent Surrender*, about what was necessary to reverse the tide of foreign control of Canadian life: "I am increasingly convinced that Canada is not going to be saved by either its academics/intellectuals as a class or its governors but by the people. If that sounds nonsense, then it is the measure of my distress, but also a measure of my resolve. I am going to the people."[1]

His "going to the people" included becoming an activist in the three major nationalist movements that formed about this time: the left-social democratic Waffle group in the New Democratic Party (1969), the Marxist Canadian Liberation Movement (1970) and the liberal Committee for an Independent Canada (1970). Though he would eventually become disillusioned with all three, he was a strong advocate in at least the first two for independent Canadian unions. That advocacy stemmed from his conception of nationalism as a force for democratic change that would benefit the common people rather than the elites. To combat the American imperialism that he argued was shackling ordinary Canadians in all aspects of their lives, he believed "there is no doubt capitalism as we know it must also be destroyed in Canada."[2] In his view, the working class would play a crucial role in combatting both imperialism and the capitalist structures that made it possible. His strong association of "the people" with the working class is apparent in his overall writing. He extolled political poetry as "poetry that makes class, capitalism, and—laterally—their implication for imperialism as it affects Canada" the focus.[3] Mathews stressed the need for Canadians to assert themselves and shed our collective "inferiority complex," saying:

---

[1] Jeffrey Cormier (30).
[2] Quoted in Misao Dean (31).
[3] Quoted in Robert Williams (8).

We have been told . . . that we are a country that should not expect to initiate ideas, to invent, to revolutionize thought or social structures. We are conditioned to be the great social gannets, picking up the scraps of social change that fall from the tables of "mature" countries. Such preaching — whatever its intentions — has served to keep our population unsure, insecure, fearful of dynamism within itself and stupidly adulatory towards the energy of other countries. We were invited to see ourselves as perpetually immature, forever needing a parent figure.[4]

From that perspective, the notion that Canadian workers needed American parent figures in their unions appeared obscene. It was just another example of "the grasp of policy-making power by Americans and by those who co-operate with the imposition of the United States reality upon Canadian reality."[5]

With his emphasis on Canadian nationalism as anti-imperialist and an effort to free Canadians to learn about and build upon their own history and culture, Mathews could hardly give a pass to American-controlled unions that were deeply tied into the American military-industrial complex where they played a leading role in attempting to crush leftist unionism in the Third World in favour of a form of unionism acceptable to American capitalists and politicians.[6]

Both the degree of American control over Canadian unions and the character of those unions were unacceptable to Mathews. He had gone to jail for organizing a protest at an Edmonton city council meeting in 1963 against the continued rule of the city by Mayor William Hawrelak, whom a judge ruled had used his position as mayor to enrich himself and his family in their private land dealings.[7] That same year, a report by Justice Thomas Norris, titled the "Industrial Inquiry Commission concerning matters related to the disruption of shipping on the Great Lakes, the St. Lawrence River system and connecting waters," detailed the thuggery of the leader of the Seafarers International Union (SIU), Hal Banks. Banks was a convicted American thug with mob connections when shipping companies on the Great Lakes hired

---

[4]   Misao Dean (37).

[5]   Robert Williams (22).

[6]   The extent of AFL-CIO collaboration with the state and corporate America in fighting union radicalism around the world had been documented by Ronald Radosh in early 1969. Later works that were able to rely on much better documentation than was available to Radosh include Kim Scipes and Anthony Carew.

[7]   Jeffrey Cormier (21).

him to form a Canadian local of the American-based SIU with the purpose of destroying the Canadian Seamen's Union (CSU). The CSU was a militant union of sailors whose officers included several active Communists. As a convicted felon, Banks was ineligible to enter Canada. The federal Liberal government turned a blind eye to Banks' past so that he could undertake a campaign of intimidation and beatings that created the appearance that a majority of sailors preferred the SIU over the CSU as their representative. The government and the primarily American-based unions in Canada condoned Banks' behaviour for about 13 years, during which he purged 2000 men from the right to work on ships and continued to rule through bullying and even murder of opponents. Only when all possibilities of the CSU recovery were long past did the government and the trade union movement move to end the mayhem for which Banks was responsible.[8]

In 1971, 77 percent of Canadian Labour Congress (CLC) affiliates were also affiliates of the AFL-CIO, the major American labour central.[9] The Canadian sections of most unions enjoyed little or no independence from the American headquarters of their unions, particularly when it came to finances. The Canadian Corporations and Labour Unions Report Act calculated that from 1962 to 1969 American unions collected $249,213,000 in Canadian worker dues, but spent only $159, 311,000 in this country. That meant a profit of $89,902,000 flowing back to the United States. That made the rate of profit for the foreign owners of Canadian unions higher than the equivalent profit rates of most foreign-owned firms in Canada.[10]

Though the argument that Canadian workers were deprived of control over their dues and their work situations by American unions seemed watertight, Mathews' nationalist allies in the Waffle leadership rejected his insistence that the organization should campaign for Canadian workers having their own unions. Both Mel Watkins and Jim Laxer regarded Mathews' request as strategically wrong. Watkins was the one-time moderate liberal economist whose government-commissioned inquiry into foreign ownership converted him to

---

[8] David Witwer documents the evidence of Banks' gangsterism as a union leader and the long-time indifference to his activities on the part of both the Canadian government and the American-union-dominated Canadian Labour Congress. Only after the CSU was gutted and Banks was regarded by the shipping companies as an extortionist rather than an anti-communist saviour did the Canadian authorities begin to investigate Banks, who then fled back to the United States.

[9] David Blocker, 2021 (56).

[10] Robert Laxer (158).

an anti-imperialist and a socialist. He had been appalled as he learned about the extent to which American control of the Canadian economy influenced a politics of subordination to American interests. Still, he resisted Mathews' argument that a similar stranglehold by American unions over Canadian workers was unacceptable. "Although we were nationalists, we did not want to take a stand denouncing international unions, despite urgings from some of our friends on the Left," Watkins said. "We felt that taking that stand would have been political suicide. For one, it would have made it impossible for us to stay in the NDP. Also, it would have put our supporters, who are militant members of international unions, in an intolerable position."[11]

Jim Laxer went further. He joined with Gerald Caplan, a founder of the Waffle who pulled away from the group relatively early on, to proclaim: "... this is no simple-minded call for the repudiation of international unionism. Only labour's enemies could seriously demand that Canadian unions voluntarily surrender their resources while powerful American-dominated multi-national corporations proliferate in Canada. But Canadian unions (should) maintain power in their own hands adequate to transform their organizations into vehicles for radical social change, with no restrictions on such activities from external forces."[12] Just how that was supposed to happen was unclear.

The Waffle embraced New Left opposition to the bureaucratic socialism that the Old Left, both communist and social democratic, had accepted. So, it called for workers, not managers, to be in charge of nationalized industries. Their manifesto in 1969 envisioned workers taking over the prerogatives of management while their unions would be run by rank-and-file workers rather than labour bureaucrats. The contradictory call for direct workers' control with a ringing defence of remaining inside foreign-controlled unions appalled Mathews. But in the eyes of Laxer and Watkins, who had closer connections with young rank-and-file unionists, it reflected solidarity with the demands of that group of unionists at the 1970 CLC convention for unions to expand collective bargaining issues to include workplace control and technological change. Those were demands that the CLC leadership responded to with hostility.[13]

Throughout the later 1960s, the hold of the union leadership over their younger members proved quite tentative as a large percentage of strikes were illegal "wildcats" that the leadership strenuously opposed. Like their American

---

[11] David Blocker, 2021 (59).
[12] Robert Hackett.
[13] Ian Milligan (32).

parent unions, their Canadian sections were committed to obeying the spirit of labour laws that in Canada were modelled on the 1944 wartime Privy Council Order 1003. That, in turn, was based on the American National Labor Relations Act of 1935, generally referred to as the Wagner Act after its principal proponent. The government would provide legal protections for unions and collective bargaining contracts in return for unions agreeing to accept management's total control over the labour process and also accepting the role of enforcer of the collective agreement. While the agreements generally provided a grievance procedure, management had many ways to stall grievances and deprive individuals and groups of a fair hearing of their complaints or their appeals against dismissals and suspensions. Wildcats were a rank-and-file response against a labour relations process that vested most power in management and made the union leaders, once an agreement was signed, guarantors of worker submissiveness. As John Lang has argued, pro-management behaviour on the part of the leaders of American branch-plant unions alienated many members and created the conditions that led to breakaways. "The driving force behind these breakaways was more a quest for democracy within the union rather than a manifestation of socialist principles or a platform for a broader critique of the economic and political relations in society."[14]

Robin Mathews regarded the American vice on Canada to be so tight that there was no time for the long-term strategic thinking of Laxer and Watkins on the American-based union issue. His faith in the people as opposed to institutions and their leaders, including those from academe, made him a supporter of breakaways and their democratic ethos. It was one of a number of issues on which Mathews was out of line with the more pragmatic Waffle leaders. While many Wafflers welcomed the support of American-born Canadian residents who opposed American imperialism, Mathews published an article in 1970 that argued that American draft dodgers needed to be viewed as bearers of American ideology.[15] He could hardly be expected to view American trade union leaders, who were pro-imperialism and sometimes exercised absolute political control over the Canadian sections of their unions, as neutral players when he viewed even clearly anti-imperialist Americans in Canada as objects of suspicion.[16]

---

[14]   John Lang (77).

[15]   Bryan Palmer (293).

[16]   I became assistant editor of *Canadian Dimension* magazine shortly after the journal's editor, Cy Gonick, published the Mathews' piece on draft dodgers. Many of our readers responded negatively to the premises of Mathews' argument. But there was abundant

Fortunately for Mathews, many younger activists in the Waffle and in the CLM agreed that the fight for Canadian unions, like the fight for Canadian ownership of industry, needed to be fought immediately. Mathews' overall influence in the Waffle paled beside that of the charismatic Laxer and the erudite Watkins, but his views could not be ignored because, as Jeffrey Cormier notes, "the name Robin Mathews, in the early stages of the movement at least, was virtually synonymous with Canadianization."[17] Activists such as John Lang, Daniel Drache, Laurell Ritchie, and Rick Salutin responded to his call to fight for sovereign Canadian unions.

The Strikes that Enhanced the Battle for Sovereign National Unions

All four were members of a reading group called the Anti-Imperialist Squad. Mathews' influence made them easy recruits when Confederation of Canadian Union organizers (CCU) Madeleine Parent and Kent Rowley attended a session of their group in 1970 where Drache and Salutin were present.[18] Parent and Rowley at once embodied the corrosive effect of Cold War American unionism in Canada that Mathews denounced and the beginnings of a Canadian nationalist response within the working class. Both were long-time trade union organizers and strike leaders in the textile industry. Since 1943, Rowley had been the Canadian director of the United Textile Workers of America (UTWA). Though neither Rowley nor Parent were members of the Communist Party, their willingness to work with Communist militants, coupled with their own militancy, proved sufficient reason for UTWA to fire both of them in 1952. They were ousted "by corrupt American leaders aided by Canadian opponents."[19] They responded by creating the Canadian

---

evidence of both arrogance and ignorance on the part of Americans regarding anti-imperialist struggles in Canada. That year (1970), for example, Gonick invited Robert Scheer, the editor of *Ramparts* magazine, the widest-circulating leftist journal in the United States, to speak in Winnipeg. As a group of us met with him after his speech, we asked his opinion about how Canadians could best go about opposing U.S. imperialism in our country. He answered that we should restrict ourselves to acting as hosts for draft dodgers, and when we spoke about our desire to fight American control of the Canadian economy and its impact on Canadian lives, his response was a guffaw.

[17] Jeffrey Cormier (20).

[18] Ian Milligan (154-5).

[19] Joan Sangster, 2012 (194). Sangster had elaborated on this issue in her 2006 article, referring to evidence in the UTWA files that reveal the plot to mislabel Rowley and Parent

Textile and Chemical Union (CTCU), which included breakaways of UTWA locals that were unhappy with their American union's apparent collaboration with management against worker interests. They went on to create the CCU in 1968 (initially named Council of Canadian Unions) as a coalition of Canadian unions that were ineligible or unwilling to be part of the American-union-dominated CLC.[20]

The Anti-Imperialist Squad Four responded positively to the couple's challenge to work with the CCU to help form Canadian unions without connections to the American unions. Drache, who would later become one of Canada's best-known left-wing nationalist scholars, was a political science student doing his MA at Queen's at the time. He was active in both the Waffle and the CLM. Salutin was a budding playwright, novelist, and journalist who would eventually become a beloved figure in the Canadian arts.

John Lang, who would embark on a lifelong career in the labour movement, was already somewhat familiar with Parent and Rowley. He was actively involved both in the Mathews-led fight for the Canadianization of the universities and in the labour movement. A contract professor at York University, his father was a Mine Mill organizer in Sudbury. While Mine Mill and United Electrical Workers were American-based unions, they were expelled from the Canadian Congress of Labour in 1949 for alleged Communist domination. Mine Mill locals faced ongoing efforts by the Steelworkers to steal their members afterwards, but held out until 1968 by implementing democratic structures of participation that challenged the accusations of their enemies that they were an authoritarian Communist union.[21] Involved in the Waffle, Lang was impressed with Mathews' strident disagreement with the Laxer-Watkins strategic defence of international unionism. Lang's involvement in the Confederation of Canadian Unions would include a 15-year stint (1978-1993) as secretary-treasurer.

Laurell Ritchie, also bound for a major career as a labour organizer with the CTCU and later as a national representative with the Canadian Auto Workers, was an anti-poverty activist and feminist. During her labour career,

---

in order to use anti-Communist hysteria to dismiss them from their union positions. She also notes that "the American UTWA leaders who ordered the dismissal were later indicted on charges of fraudulently misusing union funds" (63).

20   See the biographies of Rowley and Parent in the Notes.

21   Ron Verzuh's book is the latest effort to document the struggle by Mine Mill to survive during the Cold War in Canada. His emphasis is on British Columbia. An earlier important work on Mine Mill is the Buse-Suschnigg-Steedman book.

she was a leading member of a coalition that successfully fought for equal pay for work of equal value legislation in Ontario.

This group had become committed to the Confederation of Canadian Unions by the time a critical strike forced the Waffle to choose between the early cautious strategy of Laxer and Watkins and the strident support for Canadian unionism pressed by Robin Mathews and his supporters. The Texpack strike in Brantford, Ontario, which extended from July to October 1971, was dominated by the issue of the harm that American multinationals caused Canadian workers. Texpack was a manufacturer of medical and surgical supplies as well as industrial filters. Initially a Canadian family firm, it was bought in 1965 by American Hospital Supply. This company operated in about 100 countries and attempted to integrate its operations across the globe in ways that increased its profits regardless of the impact on workers. As Joan Sangster puts it, the Texpack takeover "meant reorganizing, downsizing, and taking a hard line on the wage bill."[22] CTCU's strategy, as summarized by Rick Salutin, was to appeal for public support "by saying this is the issue of the takeover of the Canadian economy, and they're exploiting Canadian workers, and they're putting out shoddy bandages that are going to hurt patients in Canadian hospitals because they're American bastards who don't give a shit."[23]

Eighty percent of Texpack's workers were women, many of whom were recent European immigrants, and the CTCU local that had been organized in 1958 had mainly women leaders by the time of the 1971 strike for higher wages, employment guarantees, and fairer grievance procedures. The company responded to the strike by hiring scabs (replacement workers) and using police to keep the striking workers away from the plant and the scabs. That led to violent clashes between police and strikers. Still, the Ontario Federation of Labour and the international unions refused to offer any support for the strikers because the union was affiliated with the CCU, which American-affiliated unions regarded as a threat. Many of their members, by contrast, ignored their leaders' orders to stay away from the picket line. The violent repression faced by these strikers in a strike that sharply raised the issues of the negative impacts of foreign ownership of Canadian industry strengthened the hand of Mathews and his supporters in the Waffle, who were earlier accused of being tactless hotheads. After an internal debate won by the supporters of Canadian unionism, the Waffle joined the CTCU struggle full tilt in early

---

[22]   Joan Sangster, 2006 (42).
[23]   Rick Salutin as quoted by Ian Milligan (129).

September 1971. Their presence made a big difference. While many of the Texpack workers were intimidated by the police repression, they welcomed outsiders who supported their cause and were willing to confront police efforts to protect the scabs. The Waffle Labour Committee organized a meeting of 200 Brantford union members, mostly members of internationals, on September 4, which yielded more supporters for the CTCU pickets and handled the legal fund for the strike. Many Waffle members were arrested, including Laxer and Watkins, along with Laxer's father, Robert Laxer, Daniel Drache, and Steven Penner. John Lang and Ian Lumsden, the editor of an important collection of nationalist essays, *Close the 49th Parallel: The Americanization of Canada*, were severely injured in their efforts to impede a scab bus.[24]

Though their members were clearly divided about how to respond to a strike against an exploitative American multi-national, the hostility of the leadership of the international unions to the CTCU permitted the Textile Workers Union of America (TWUA) to collaborate with the Texpack bosses to reopen an unused Texpack plant in Toronto. That was clearly part of the management's policy to break the union using any means possible, and the TWUA provided a fig leaf for company strategy by accepting the management's offer to represent Toronto scabs. This created friction within the CLC. The Canadian Union of Public Employees, whose leaders included Canadian nationalists, who were sympathetic to wholly Canadian unions, demanded that the CLC intervene in the Texpack strike on behalf of the CTCU. While a member of the American-union-dominated and almost exclusively male CLC, CUPE was an independent Canadian union whose members were mostly women. Its officers were increasingly women as well, and Grace Hartman, secretary-treasurer since 1967 and president after 1975, was both a nationalist and a feminist.

Joan Sangster, examining the Texpack strike, writes: "While criticisms can be made of the political analysis of Left nationalist organizing over 30 years ago, its legacy included an energetic militancy, a coherent commitment to a socialist transformation, and an optimistic belief in the possibility of the working class's ability to change the world. All those are worth remembering in our current struggle."[25]

But if the Texpack victory animated the nationalist Left that Mathews had played a significant role in creating, it completely alienated the American-

---

[24] Joan Sangster, 2006 (47).
[25] Joan Sangster, 2006 (62).

based unions from the Waffle. The success of the strike challenged the narrative of the internationals that Canadian breakaways could not muster the strength to defeat multi-national corporations in a labour conflict. The Waffle Labour Committee added insult to injury by organizing a large contingent for the Ontario Federation of Labour convention in November, 1971 to reinforce the demands of radicals within the American-headquartered unions for full Canadian autonomy, including an end to union dues being sent to the United States. Such Waffle interventions in favour of grassroots control over the leadership of Canadian sections of the American-controlled unions led to those unions pressuring Steven Lewis to muzzle the Waffle. Lewis understood their demands as an unstated ultimatum that international union funds, upon which the Ontario NDP depended, would not be forthcoming if he failed to take decisive action. Lewis accused the Waffle of being a "party within a party" and ordered the Waffle to either disband as a formal group or leave the party.[26]

The Manitoba Waffle, concerned with the national impact of the Ontario situation on the Waffle, invited Ontario representatives and other provincial Waffle representatives to a conference in Winnipeg on the future of the Waffle in March 1972. Robin Mathews was to be part of the Ontario delegation, but because of illness, he asked his wife Esther to replace him. Esther, as confidential minutes of the meetings showed, confronted Trotskyists within the Waffle who challenged the nationalist agenda and who suggested that the Waffle's calls for union autonomy and breakaways were a distraction from the fight for international socialism. By then, the Waffle leadership agreed with Robin and Esther Mathews and decided to take the Waffle outside the NDP rather than disband.[27]

That, in turn, contributed to decisions by Waffle groups across the country to leave the NDP. The majority group in the Ontario Waffle reconstituted itself as the Movement for an Independent Socialist Canada, while the Trotskyists formed the Revolutionary Marxist Group. Though Laxer was clear that members of MISC could, if they choose, also remain NDP members, the Waffle lost a large group of their former members when they departed the NDP. The successor organizations to the Waffle proved short-lived.

---

[26] David Blocker, 2019 (323-4).

[27] David Blocker, 2019 (317). John Warnock and I wrote the "notes on a clandestine and unofficial meeting of provincial Waffle representatives and interested observers" to which Blocker makes reference.

It is impossible to know whether continuing to pursue the more cautious approach to the unions that Laxer and Watkins had originally advocated might have allowed the Waffle to eventually become the dominant force in the NDP. Laxer had won 37 percent of the federal leadership vote against David Lewis on the final ballot in 1971and the Waffle had considerable strength within a number of the provincial parties. Texpack or not, neither David or Stephen Lewis nor the international unions were likely to have countenanced a potential Waffle takeover, and a takeover might in any case have left the NDP without the union base that provided its financial support. In any case, ousting the Waffle from the NDP and then the gradual disappearance of the Waffle weakened but did not destroy either the nationalist Left nor the movement to create a national-controlled union movement. The momentum that Robin Mathews and his supporters had helped to activate penetrated the consciousness of Canadian workers. Demands for greater autonomy within American-based unions swelled, as well as the breakaway movements that gained ground throughout the 1970s and afterwards.

Continued CCU militancy led the way by showing what determined independent Canadian unions could achieve for workers in small plants, often mainly employing women and largely ignored by the big American unions, especially when community support could be organized to help the strikers. In 1972, it was the turn of 100 members belonging to the CCU-affiliated Union of Professional and Clerical Employees, Local 574, at Dare Cookies in Kitchener to challenge the idea that women workers could be paid "pin money" rather than a family wage. In 1973, came the CTCU strike of about 115 primarily male immigrant workers at picture frame manufacturer Artistic Woodwork in Toronto. It was a 4-month bitter strike featuring "ritualized violence daily." One historian claims it symbolized "the widespread turn toward Marxism and the working class as a necessary component of social change; the importance of nationalism as a unifying factor; and the continuing social responsibility of the student and the intellectual."[28] Workers from Latin America and Greece among the strikers had a tradition of resistance that contributed to the determination of the strikers to hold out against a brutal employer. Mathews-inspired leaders were largely running the show after Kent Rowley suffered a stroke. John Lang notes: "members of the Company of Canadians, such as Rick Salutin, Daniel Drache and myself, took over,

---

[28]   Ian Milligan (151).

and together with Madeleine, started organizing workers."[29] They were also responsible for recruiting hundreds of left-wing individuals to join the daily picket line that braved police attacks.

Similar support was provided in Manitoba to strikes led by the Canadian Association of Industrial, Mechanical and Allied Workers (CAIMAW) in Manitoba. CAIMAW was formed as a breakaway from the International Molders and Foundry Union in Winnipeg in 1964. When I interviewed its president, Pat McEvoy, for an article on CAIMAW for *Canadian Dimension* in 1971, he explained that the union was formed because many members felt that the international union simply transferred their dues to their American headquarters and provided no service to the members. CAIMAW, which joined the CCU, led several important strikes. Support staff of the University of Manitoba, who organized a union for the first time in 1969, chose to join CAIMAW the following year. In October 1973, the female-dominated union went on strike for higher wages. CLC member unions provided no direct support, but some of their members joined many students in staffing the picket lines of a strike that proved successful after the union's power plant maintenance workers threatened to leave it idle as Manitoba's cold winter began to settle in.

More important politically was the long and violent Griffin foundry strike that began in September 1976 with wages and fringe benefits in play, but the company's insistence on compulsory overtime became the key issue. The mostly elderly male workforce found the long hours of demanding blue-collar work excruciating. The violence began when Griffin reopened five months after the strike began with strike-breakers whose entry into the plant was accompanied by police. Many unionists, with or without the support of their union, joined the Griffin strikers in efforts to prevent the scabs from taking their jobs. During a 6-week period, 370 strikers and their supporters were arrested before the courts restricted the size of the picket line, effectively handing a victory to management.[30] While the entire labour movement had been pressuring the NDP government of Ed Schreyer to ban compulsory overtime for several years, the CLC asked its affiliates not to provide financial support to the CAIMAW local at Griffin, putting their hatred of breakaway unions above the needs of the workers. That limited the pressure on Schreyer to change his mind about the need for a ban on obligatory overtime work.[31]

---

[29]   John Lang (81).

[30]   See Errol Black.

[31]   "The CCU and the CLC: Two Very Different Labour Centrals." *CAIMAW Review*, n.d.

Disillusionment with Schreyer's intransigence significantly reduced the number of volunteers available to the NDP in the provincial election in the fall of 1977, an election that the NDP lost. Nationalist unions were also expanding and forming in British Columbia. The Independent Pulp and Paper Workers of Canada, formed in 1963, became founding members of the CCU. In the 1970s they were joined as independent Canadian unions in that province by the Canadian Association of Smelter and Allied Workers (CASAW) and by the feminist Service, Office and Retail Workers' Union of Canada (SORWUC).[32]

Changes were also occurring inside the CLC. The growth of public service unions, virtually all independent Canadian unions, changed the arithmetic at conventions in favour of Canadian-controlled unions. In 1973, the CLC convention had voted to spend a million dollars to combat breakaways. But one year later, responding to the nationalist concerns of critics like Robin Mathews, the four major public service unions put forward guidelines for autonomy to be provided to Canadian sections of American-based unions. As more and more CLC executive positions fell to the Canadian unions, a rift developed that caused the construction unions, whose Canadian sections lacked much in the way of autonomy from American headquarters, to abandon the CLC.[33] Meanwhile breakaways from American-based unions mounted: the Communication Workers in 1972 followed by Paperworkers, 1974, Brewery Workers, 1974, Energy and Chemical Workers, 1980, Woodworkers, 1986, and most significantly given the size of their membership, Autoworkers, 1986.[34]

While the CLC did not become a voice for the kind of socialist Canada that either Robin Mathews or the Waffle leaders envisioned, they embraced Canadian nationalism sufficiently to hire Mel Watkins to research and then write the CLC brief to federal legislators on the proposed Free Trade Agreement that Brian Mulroney legislated after winning the 1988 federal election.[35] In the years that followed, however, the trade union movement, though more Canadianized, did not provide consistent support for a national industrial policy.[36] The hegemonic impact of neo-liberalism translated into

---

[32] On SORWUC, see Julia Smith.

[33] Laxer provides the details of the changing complexion of the CLC as the 1970s progressed.

[34] Gilbert Levine., "The Waffle and the Labour Movement," *Studies in Political Economy* (Autumn 1990): 185-192.

[35] Andrew Jackson.

[36] The CLC's acceptance of free trade with the Americans despite all the job losses that the Free Trade Agreement of 1989 entailed is analyzed in "Editorial: Canadian Dimenson."

a rollback in nationalist sentiment, though undoubtedly, many voices in the trade union movement would continue to echo the views of Robin Mathews on the need for greater Canadian control over our country's economy.

Conclusion

Writing to Brian Fawcett in 1976, Robin Mathews wrote: "My work was to give Canadians their rights to jobs (as Germans, Russians, Hungarians, English, etc. have those rights). That is not cultural nationalism. My work was to permit young Canadians to learn seriously about their own history, culture and political-economic-social milieu. That is not cultural nationalism. My work was to resist imperialism."[37] It was only natural that he would insist that an anti-imperialist project in Canada must include an autonomous Canadian union movement that would fight for jobs, speak to its members about their national milieu rather than its American counterpart, and "resist imperialism." He hoped that such unions would contribute to his vision of a socialist Canada where Canadian voices would cease to be muffled. His influence on young activists whose backgrounds included both New Left opposition to both bureaucratic Communist visions of socialism and the tepid prescriptions of mainline social democrats was immense. They, in turn, worked with socialist unionists of an earlier generation, like Madeleine Parent and Kent Rowley, to create a militant, nationalist trade union movement with a socialist bent. Their efforts were a partial success. While many American-based unions survive in Canada to the present day, they now account for less than a quarter of trade union members in Canada, and many now enjoy a fair degree of autonomy from their American parents.[38] But the trade union movement, as it has evolved in Canada since Mathews' time, while it could be a leading force in a revived nationalist movement, does not appear terribly interested in assuming that mantle. It has, however, moved beyond Cold War blind support for American foreign policy and has worked closely with a variety of grassroots social movements for progressive change far more than it found comfortable during the period when American-based unions ran the trade union show in Canada.

In the more recent renegotiation of the North American Free Trade Agreement, the CLC attempted to gain concessions for Canadian labour but not to dismantle free trade as such. See "Canadian Labour Congress."

[37] Misao Dean (31).

[38] See Steven Tufts.

Works Cited

Black, Errol. "'In Search of Industrial Harmony': The Process of Labour Law Reform in Manitoba, 1984." *Relations Industrielles/Industrial Relations* 1 (1985), 140-161.

Blocker, David. "Labour and the Waffle: Unions Confront Left Nationalism in the New Democratic Party." *Labour/Le Travail* 87 (Spring 2021): 49-92.

Blocker, David G. " 'To Waffle to the Left:?' The Waffle, the New Democratic Party, and Canada's Left During the Long Sixties," PhD thesis, Western University, 2019.

Buse, Dieter K., Peter Suschnigg, and Mercedes Steedman. *Hard Lessons: The Mine Mill Union in the Canadian Labour Movement.* Toronto, Dundurn, 1995.

Canadian Labour Congress. "NAFTA Renegotiation." https://canadianlabour.ca/uncategorized/nafta-renegotiation-opportunity-more-fairness/ retrieved 14 November, 2023.

Carew, Anthony. *American Labour's Cold War Abroad: From Deep Freeze to Détente, 1945-1970.* Edmonton, Athabasca University Press, 2018.

"The CCU and the CLC: Two Very Different Labour Centrals." *CAIMAW Review,* n.d.chrome-extension://efaidnbmnnnibpcajpcglclefindmkaj/https://open.library.ubc.ca/media/stream/pdf/auce/1.0377112/7 retrieved 12 November, 2023.

Cormier, Jeffrey. *The Canadianization Movement: Emergence, Survival, and Success.* Toronto, University of Toronto Press, 2004.

Dean, Misao. "Canadianization, Colonialism, and Decolonization: Investigating the Legacy of 'Seventies Nationalism' in the Robin Mathews Fonds." *Studies in Canadian Literature* 41, 1 (2016):27-48.

"Editorial: CLC Policy on the Trading Block." *Canadian Dimension,* November 1, 2004. https://canadiandimension.com/articles/view/clc-policy-on-the-trading-block-editorial

Hackett, Robert. "Pie in the Sky: A History of the Ontario Waffle." *Canadian Dimension,* October/November, 1980. reprinted on-line on 29 December, 2021. https://canadiandimension.com/articles/view/pie-in-the-sky-a-history-of-the-ontario-waffle. Retrieved 9 November, 2023.

Jackson, Andrew. "Mel Watkins: A Life Well Lived." *Canadian Dimension,* 3 April, 2020. https://canadiandimension.com/articles/view/mel-watkins-a-life-well-lived. Retrieved 13 November, 2023.

Lang, John, "Carrying on the Struggle in Ontario: 152-1973." in Andrée Lévesque. *Madeleine Parent, Activist.* Toronto, Sumach, 2005.

Laxer, Robert. *Canada's Unions*. Toronto, James Lorimer, 1976.

Levine, Gilbert. "The Waffle and the Labour Movement." *Studies in Political Economy* 33 (Autumn 1990): 185-192.

Milligan, Ian. *Rebel Youth: 1960s Labour Unrest, Young Workers and New Leftists in Canada*. Vancouver, UBC Press, 2014.

Palmer, Bryan D. *Canada's 1960s: The Ironies of Identity in a Rebellious Era*. Toronto, University of Toronto Press, 2009.

Radosh, Ronald. *American Labor and United States Foreign Policy: The Cold War in the Unions*. New York, Random House, 1969.

Salutin, Rick. *Kent Rowley: The Organizer: A Canadian Union Life*. Toronto, James Lorimer, 1980

Sangster, Joan. "Historical Legacies: Madeleine Parent." *Labour/Le Travail* 70 (Fall 2012): 193-199.

Sangster, Joan. "Remembering Texpack: Nationalism, Internationalism and Militancy in Canadian Unions." *Studies in Political Economy* 78 (Fall 2006): 41-66.

Scipes, Kim. *AFL-CIO's Secret War Against Developing Country Workers: Solidarity or Sabotage*. Lanham, MD, Lexington Books, 2011.

Smith, Julia. "An 'Entirely Different' Kind of Union: The Service, Office, and Retail Workers' Union of Canada (SORWUC), 1972-1986." *Labour/Le Travail*, 73 (Spring 2014): 23-65.

Tufts, Steven. "It's Time for Canada's Unions to Work More Clearly with U.S. Counterparts." *The Globe and Mail*, 22 October, 2023.

Verzuh, Ron. *Smelter Wars: A Rebellious Red Trade Union Fights for Its Life in Wartime Western Canada*. Toronto: University of Toronto Press, 2022.

Williams, Robert. "Robin Mathews and the Canadian Dialectic: Forms of Nationalist Thought in Canada." MA thesis, University of Northern British Columbia, 2005.

Witwer, David. "The Jimmy Hoffa of Canada: Hal Banks and a Comparative Perspective on Union Corruption." *Labour/Le Travail* 89 (Spring 2022): 27-60.

GREAT CANADIAN THEATRE COMPANY: IN THE BEGINNING

By Bill Law

The reviews were terrible for a new play called *For Love, Quebec*. The playwright was Robin Mathews. I was the director. It was not a very good play, nor a very strong cast and my direction did nothing to save the situation.[1] We were in the kitchen at the back of Robin and Esther's home on Fourth Avenue in Ottawa. With the newspapers scattered about and the scathing comments hanging in the air, I said, "God, Robin, this is awful." He looked me in the eye and told me to forget the reviews. "The important thing is that the company carries on, that it survives." That was January 1978. Now, nearly 50 years later, GCTC (The Great Canadian Theatre Company), though a long way from its leftist, agitprop, and cultural nationalist beginnings, is still standing.

Robin was a charismatic and fiery teacher who attracted those students, like me, who had come of age in the late 1960s and were searching for mentors, ones that shared our anti-capitalist and cultural nationalist yearnings for a Canada and a Canadian university system that was not dependent on foreign lecturers who too often ignored Canadian narratives and denied us our cultural legitimacy. Students considered to be of some promise were told, as I was, that to study Canadian literature was to throw away a career. The university building boom of the sixties had filled academia with British and American expats, many of undoubted quality, some of dubious merit. Most of those recruited into university English Departments had no grasp of or interest in Canadian literature, which, if it was considered at all, was

---

[1] The play, a fictionalized account of the kidnapping of a British diplomat by the FLQ had been a subject of disagreement between myself as director, Larry McDonald the artistic director and Robin. As detailed by Scott Duchesne in his PhD thesis on the early days of the company we had written a detailed letter to Robin laying out our objections about the play justifying murder in the cause of liberation. As I recall Robin did modify his position in subsequent rewrites. See Scott Duchesne, "'Fitful Excellence: The Great Canadian Theatre Company and English-Speaking Theatre in Ottawa, 1975-1983." PhD dissertation, University of Toronto, 2004. p .166.

considered inferior. Robin was the angry, articulate voice of resistance who had already done much to challenge the openly colonialist ideology then still prevalent in our universities. More than anyone else, he had opened the door to jobs for Canadian academics in Canadian universities, a crucial building block to putting Canadian literature into the curricula.

In the mid-seventies, I was a graduate student at Ottawa's Carleton University, where in 1968, Robin, together with James Steele, another professor in the English Department, had launched their campaign.[2] At the time, I was described by my then girlfriend, not unkindly, it must be said, as a "crude Marxist." I had an ill-defined sense of what it meant to be a Canadian but a very clear idea of what I considered to be right and what was wrong. As an undergraduate at the University of Guelph, I had been part of a small group that protested Pierre Elliot Trudeau's invocation of the 1970 War Measures Act, the infamous "state of apprehended insurrection." That politically ruthless and legally questionable use of martial law, I believed then and still believe, was an extraordinary abuse of power. Coming into Robin's orbit, I was, I suppose, something of a rebel with a cause that lacked a clear definition. Robin was to give the cause shape. His reputation was such that when I returned to university at Carleton, it was inevitable I would find myself taking his Can Lit seminars.

He was a gifted teacher with a sardonic wit sometimes tinged with contempt. He was demanding in his expectations, and those who came ill-prepared paid the consequence. But he was also enormously kind and generous and his and his wife Esther's home on Fourth Avenue in Ottawa's Glebe district was always open to students. It was at one such gathering that the conversation turned to the creation of a theatre company that would champion left-wing Canadian content and only Canadian content: playwrights, actors, directors, designers, front and back of house. As I recall, there were four of us in that conversation in the spring of 1975: Robin, myself and two other graduate students, Greg Reid and Lois Shannon.

Greg and I had just concluded the season of the Carleton University drama society, Sock' n' Buskin. Inspired by Robin we'd embarked the previous September on a mandate to do a run of Canadian plays. That decision had a backdrop. I was approached by the drama society to take over as president and fight to preserve funding from being cut by the student council president,

---

2 Robin Mathews and James Steele, editors *The Fight for Canadian Universities*, New Press, 1969.

an engineering student whose idea of culture, she told me, was to build a concrete canoe and float it down the Rideau River that runs beside the campus. My terms to Sock' n' Buskin were that I would take the job, argue before student council for the funding and when it was secured, the society would commit to delivering a season of Canadian plays. In the event, we won by one vote when a council member whose claim to notoriety was to abstain on every issue took his full measure of fleeting fame to ponder for what seemed an agonizingly long time before voting yes to break a tie and renew the funding.

The all-Canadian season - something I am sure I am right in saying had never before been done anywhere in Canada - proved wildly successful with two premieres, a musical, two one-act plays and a children's play. The musical, an adaptation of Stephen Leacock's *Sunshine Sketches of a Little Town*, packed the 400-seat Alumni Theatre. Other shows drew similarly robust crowds. One of the premieres was Robin's play *A Woman is Dying*, and the other was Gerry Potter's *Chaudiere Strike*. Lois Shannon directed *A Woman is Dying*, a play that looking back after all these years, strikes me now as both cryptic and dreary. *Chaudiere Strike*, written by a fellow graduate student, Gerry Potter, told the story of how workers at the vast E.B. Eddy paper mill in Hull struck and unionized at the turn of the 20th century. It was a play with much more punch and narrative direction to it, but such was the strength of Robin's charismatic hold that none of us doubted that *A Woman is Dying* was a piece of theatrical brilliance.

Robin believed emphatically that he could and would do anything to advance the cause of cultural nationalism. That belief was infectious. He could, for example, take a dreary novel of the 19th century and convince us that it was a lost Canadian masterpiece, victim of the cultural imperialism inflicted upon us by the British and, latterly and most egregiously, by America. For him to sit down and write a play at speed, which he did with *A Woman is Dying*, never having written a play before, was a statement and an act of cultural liberation. He empowered us by doing so, and the doing of it was enough to convince us of the merits of the play.

Arthur Milner, who later became GCTC's writer-in-residence and then artistic director, joined the company in the autumn of 1975. He recalls that "Robin believed he could do these things, and they needed to be done. And, therefore, he was the one to do them in order to feed that dream of creating a vibrant Canadian cultural scene."[3] That we didn't see the flaws, that we were

---

[3]   Author's interview with Arthur Milner, November 15, 2023.

caught up in his charisma, is, on reflection, a good thing. Had we paused for thought, we would not have carried our belief in a Canadian cultural revolution forward. None of us had any formal theatre training and had we reflected on just how green and ignorant we were in the art of theatre, GCTC would not have seen the light of day. Robin proposed that in order to launch the company, each of us should contribute $1500, a huge amount of money for impoverished students. We accepted without questioning that it was one thing for a tenured university professor to come up with the money and quite another for his students to do so. I borrowed most of mine from my parents and I don't suppose I ever paid it back. It was Robin's way of testing our commitment to the revolution.

The theatre company quickly recruited supporters to the cause. Once a month on Sundays, members would gather at Robin and Esther's home for conversations, assessments, ideas on fundraising and political debate, within a framework driven by his vision of an independent socialist Canada that must rid itself of U.S. cultural and economic imperialism. The meetings were both invigorating and draining, an example of the latter being a long and drawn-out debate about whether landed immigrants could become members of the company, sparked by the request of someone born in the U.S. who wanted to join GCTC. In the end, after a huge wrangle with Robin, it was decided by a vote that landed immigrants on a path to Canadian citizenship could sign up.

GCTC was born into an English-language theatrical landscape in Ottawa that could best be described as largely barren of Canadian content. The Ottawa Little Theatre was proudly amateur and utterly disdainful of Canadian plays and playwrights. As a local theatre critic approvingly wrote in 1975, "The repertoire is a tried-and-true mixture of comedies, farces, thrillers and classic dramas. Coarse language is rare, as are controversial subjects."[4] Its 1975 summer season featured Henrik Ibsen's *An Enemy of the People*, Noel Coward's *Blithe Spirit* and Neil Simon's *The Prisoner of Second Avenue*. The National Arts Centre[5] had opened its doors in 1969 with George Ryga's *The Ecstasy of Rita Joe*, a searing and seminal play about a young Indigenous woman whose short life ends when she is raped and murdered by three white men. (When it opened

---

[4]   Scott Duchesne, '"Fitful Excellence: The Great Canadian Theatre Company and English-Speaking Theatre in Ottawa, 1975-1983," PhD dissertation, University of Toronto, 2004, p .67.

[5]   James Noonan, 'The National Arts Centre: Fifteen Years at Play', 1985 Theatre Research in Canada v6 n1 (198501): 56-81 https://journals.lib.unb.ca/index.php/tric/article/view/7430/8489

in Washington DC in 1973 *The Ecstasy of Rita Joe* was roasted by the theatre critic of the New York Times who sneeringly began his review "Canadian playwright. The words seem a little incongruous together, like 'Panamanian hockey⬜player,' almost, or 'Lebanese fur trapper.'")[6]

It took three years before another Canadian play hit centre stage at the NAC, David Freeman's *Battering Ram*. It was followed in 1973 with Theatre Passe Muraille's touring version of *The Farm Show*. However, in the 1974-75 English theatre season,[7] the NAC offered a quartet of Canadian plays: the Toronto Workshop Production of Barry Broadfoot's *Ten Lost Years*, John Coulter's *Riel*, James Reaney's *Killdeer* and David Fennario's *On the Job*.

The Toronto theatre scene presented quite a different story. In 1959, George Luscombe founded Toronto Workshop Productions, which is considered to be the granddaddy of Canada's alternative theatre scene. Other companies followed its path of leftist, participatory and collective theatre-making.

By the time GCTC was launched, Toronto's alternative scene was alive and thriving with a mix of foreign and Canadian content. Chief among the companies was Theatre Passe Muraille, founded by Jim Garrard in 1968. Garrard was part of Rochdale College, an alternative educational movement and free university, which by the time of its closure in 1975, had secured a notorious reputation, described by the CBC as "North America's largest drug distribution warehouse."[8] Theatre Passe Muraille's first production was *Futz*, an exploration of a sexual relationship between a woman and a pig by the New York playwright and poet Rochelle Owens. It secured for the fledgling company instant notoriety after being shut down by the police on the grounds of obscenity and outraging public decency.

Toronto Free Theatre was another company launched in 1971 with the broadcaster and journalist (and subsequently Canadian Governor General) Adrienne Clarkson among its original board of directors. As described by the *Oxford Companion to Canadian Theatre*: "the theatre would be free both in its admission policy and in the sense of experimentation with, and ideological

---

6   Julius Novick 'Ecstasy: The Indian's Agony' The New York Times May 13, 1973. https://www.nytimes.com/1973/05/13/archives/ecstasy-the-indians-agony-theater-in-washington-dc.html

7   Noonan, "The National Arts Centre: Fifteen Years at Play."

8   Rochdale   College   https://en.wikipedia.org/wiki/Rochdale_College#:~:text=According%20to%20the%20CBC%20Archives,the%20beginning%20of%20the%20end.

exploration of, all avenues of theatrical expression, especially those followed by Canadian theatrical artists."[9] True to the founding ethos, TFT opened with a play by the Canadian author and playwright Tom Hendry, who had co-founded the company with Martin Kinch and John Palmer.

Ken Gass who had moved from Abbotsford BC to Toronto in 1968 set up Factory Theatre Lab as a hothouse for Canadian playwrights. As he put it in language that echoed Robin: "By limiting the Factory to only new Canadian plays, we were forced to abandon the security blanket of our colonial upbringing."[10] Among the playwrights he developed and who went on to have significant careers were David Fennario and George F. Walker. Tarragon Theatre was another launched at the end of the sixties, focusing on Canadian plays and playwrights. The founders, the husband and wife team of Bill Glassco and Jane Gordon, intended Tarragon to be a "a showcase for new Canadian plays interpreted by Canadian theatre artists" with an emphasis on "plays to which (Glassco) could give the best possible productions so that a new audience could also be found and nurtured."[11] The company opened to critical and audience acclaim with David Freeman's *Creeps*.

Theatre Pass Muraille, after opening with *Futz*, went on to produce Canadian plays in the early seventies, among them *The Farm Show* and Carol Bolt's *Buffalo Jump*, which tells the story of the 1935 On to Ottawa protest march at the height of the Great Depression. In 1977, GCTC mounted a new version of *Buffalo Jump* that Bolt and the company had jointly reworked and which I directed. Bolt was a founding member of Playwrights Co-op, set up in 1971 to catalogue Canadian plays and promote their production. Playwrights Co-op had already proved its worth to me in that Carleton University all-Canadian theatre season that became the catalyst for GCTC.

It was a tradition that Carleton's Sock 'n' Buskin produced a children's play in December. The student director, an American, announced that as there were "no Canadian children's plays," she had chosen one from her homeland. I called Bolt and asked her to send me six Canadian plays, which I then gave to the director, who, after the most cursory reads, declared none was good enough to produce. I rounded up my executive, and we resigned

---

[9]   Eugene Benson and L.W. Conolly, *The Oxford Companion to Canadian Theatre*, Oxford University Press, 1989 p. 556.

[10]   Gaetan Charlebois 'Factory Theatre', The Canadian Theatre Encyclopedia. https://www.canadiantheatre.com/dict.pl?term=Factory%20Theatre

[11]   Keith Garebian, Urjo Kareda 'Tarragon Theatre', The Canadian Encyclopedia. https://www.thecanadianencyclopedia.ca/en/article/tarragon-theatre

en masse. The director quickly lowered the American flag and chose one of the Canadian plays to do. It was an outcome that delighted Robin.

His ideological core was shaped by a deep resistance to and resentment of American cultural influences, which he saw within a broader context of the struggle against U.S. imperialism and what he regarded as a comprador liberal ruling elite in Canada that assisted in the process of cultural colonization. In his 2004 doctoral thesis on the early history of GCTC (1975-1983), Scott Duchesne argues the following:

"For Mathews, the success or the failure of the Great Canadian Theatre Company depended on its opposition to, or its complicity with perpetuating what he called the 'liberal ideology,' the dominant philosophy that, according to him, had robbed Canada of its opportunity to develop into its own unique culture and had allowed the dominant cultures of imperialist nations to subsume the national culture and define what it was to be "Canadian."[12]

That Robin saw GCTC as a weapon in the cultural war upon which he was embarked goes a long way to explaining the extraordinarily hostile reception the company received from Ottawa's small band of established theatre critics, two of whom were expats, the Ottawa Citizen's Audrey Ashley and the Carleton University English professor Charles Haines, the former from Britain and the latter from the United States. The critics ruthlessly zeroed in on our numerous production weaknesses and the failings of ill-trained actors and directors. They took exception to the name of the company, which we intended to be both ironic and a bold statement of intent. They didn't like our fundraising buttons proclaiming "GCTC: Pure Canadian Talent." The slogan was a cheeky play on maple syrup marketing, but the critics saw it as xenophobic and racist. They were not going to cut any slack for a group of what they saw as ideologically driven amateurs flogging a brand of agitprop theatre they detested.

From our side of the stage, we were learning on the fly while using overtly political messaging to attack what we saw as the sacred cows of Western imperialist capitalism and cultural subjugation. Small wonder our flight path took us directly into the gun sights of the established critics. As Duchesne puts it: "On some level, I believe that the members of the Great Canadian Theatre Company under the influence of Robin Mathews, like many of those involved

---

[12]   Scott Duchesne 'Fitful Excellences: The Great Canadian Theatre Company and English-speaking Ottawa Theatre, 1975-1983 PhD thesis, University of Toronto 2004. National Library of Canada, ISBN: 0-612-91728-2 p. 34.

in the cultural nationalist movement in English Canada, were extraordinarily naive regarding the effects of the language they were employing."[13] Looking back, after all these years, I cannot say I disagree with that assessment. But there was strength in that naivete, and Robin simply would not let the negative reviews drag us down. Rather, he used the reviews to fire the struggle.

Typical of the lashings that the company was to receive in its early years was this from the *Ottawa Journal* review of GCTC's first-ever production, Herschel Hardin's *Esker Mike and His Wife Agiluk*:

"I didn't hate all of the production of the play by a new group ludicrously named The Great Canadian Theatre Company, but I hated a lot of it. ... even as an amateur production, the actors showed an almost complete lack of awareness of such things as nuance, shading, movement and speaking properly. ... As a group the players were unconvincing, inadequate, sloppy, and embarrassing."[14]

Arthur Milner recalls how two other companies that came onto the Ottawa scene shortly after the GCTC were much more favourably viewed by the critics: "We were disparaged as dour Marxist-Leninists, nationalists, Maoists, whatever, who cared only about politics and not at all about good theatre and art. Penguin was regarded as a serious artistic company, Theatre 2000 as the gutsy innovative company."[15] Neither Penguin Theatre Company nor Theatre 2000 was to survive.

Patrick McDonald, another early recruit to GCTC who went on to serve as artistic director from 1981 to 1987, recalls the critics consistently asking, 'Why is GCTC so political? Why does it have to be Canadian?'

"Penguin was art, Theatre 2000 was art. GCTC was politics masquerading as theatre. And yet, we're the company that did survive. And people have often asked me why. We survived because we had the strongest mandate and the spine of the mandate was Canadian and political." [16]

It was Robin who gave the company the ideological structure for that spine. One wonders if, had he returned as a professor to the University of Toronto from whence he had graduated (and where he had crossed swords with Northrup Frye) and launched his culture offensive in an already febrile and innovative Toronto theatre scene, whether GCTC would have seen

---

[13]   Ibid., p. 42.

[14]   Noonan, "The National Arts Centre: Fifteen Years at Play."

[15]   Author's interview with Arthur Milner.

[16]   Author's interview with Patrick McDonald, December 6, 2023.

the light of day, let alone survive. As much as he was a builder, he was an iconoclast. He sought out fights and expected complete loyalty to a cause he largely defined. You were either with him or against him, but either way, his impact was enormous on those who were pulled into and then spun out of his orbit. McDonald credits Robin for enabling his long and successful career in Canadian theatre. He describes him fondly as "the grandfather" of the cultural nationalism movement:

"Robin was the backbone, and I will be forever thankful for that. Because it really opened my eyes to what it meant to be Canadian. Just what it meant to be Canadian. Where Robin was short with people it was because he also wanted you to share his exact political worldview. And so, it was difficult if you strayed from that. It was hard for him to separate cultural nationalism from a real left-wing view of the world." [17]

Despite its long string of producing original Canadian theatre, GCTC never cracked the Toronto market in any serious way. A sympathetic view would be that Toronto, being Toronto, viewed Ottawa (and the rest of English Canada), as Patrick McDonald puts it, as a cultural hinterland: "It was very, very Canadian. You know, if you're outside of Toronto, you're the hinterland. You might be doing some interesting things, but you're just an outpost."[18] No doubt, there is that element of snobbery that anyone who has lived and worked in Toronto and then moved to another Canadian city can attest to. But perhaps equally, too, the rigid ideological structure that Robin enforced on GCTC with its political imperative overriding concerns about the quality of scripts, direction and performance provided sufficient reason for Toronto to sniff dismissively.

I left Ottawa and the theatre world in 1979.[19] Robin remained a potent force, but increasingly, in the 1980s, his worldview and the views of the board began to diverge. It didn't help that he was a proud man who did not take kindly to criticism of his writing. Milner recalls working with Robin on a children's play about the town of Port Hope where in 1975 extremely high levels of radon gas were found in a primary school built above a nuclear waste dump site. Robin wrote the play and gave it to the board, which at the time included himself, Milner, Patrick McDonald and his older brother Larry McDonald, like Robin,

---

[17]   Ibid.
[18]   Author's interview with Patrick McDonald.
[19]   GCTC Newsletter, May 1979, LW Conolly Theatre Archives, University of Guelph Library
      https://www.lib.uoguelph.ca/archives/our-collections/lw-conolly-theatre-archives/great-
      canadian-theatre-company/

a professor in Carleton University's English Department and a GCTC actor and director and artistic director. All four had previously worked collaboratively and very successfully on a play called *Sandinista!* about Daniel Ortega and the Nicaragua revolution. Robin was not especially happy about a play without a Canadian subject, but he was mollified by the thought that Ortega had struck a mighty blow against U.S. imperialism. The children's play about a radioactive school proved a far less happy collaboration, as Milner recounts:

> Robin decided to write that story and everybody was okay with that and Larry was going to direct it. But when we got the script from Robin, he gave it to us to read and we just thought it was pretty bad. And we joked about it, calling it Two Kids Speak. Eight Men Speak had been a legendary play in Canadian theatre history, produced by the Communist Party and shut down by the police. And I think every leftist theatre company, when they heard about Eight Men Speak, said, 'Hey, let's produce that play. That would be fantastic.' And I know in our case, we read it and went, 'God, we can't produce this. It's just awful.' So, that was a pretty disparaging thing to say about his play.[20]

Stung by the joke and upset with the suggestions made to improve the play, Robin wrote a lengthy letter to the board critiquing each and every suggestion and dismissing them as ridiculous. He accused the company of selling out the story. As remembered by Milner, he was "angry but pretending not to be, and he said you take it and you do what you want with it." That was the end of Robin's active engagement with GCTC. There were no more Sunday evening meetings at his Fourth Avenue home.

By then, the GCTC had its own space, a disused warehouse, and it had become an equity company. The building proved to be an expensive undertaking, one that required drawing good houses to survive. That meant varying the fare by introducing less overtly political material onto the menu whilst still sticking to the mandate of Canadian plays. It was not a shift that Robin was at all accepting about or comfortable with. Patrick McDonald describes it as a major reason for Robin's rupture from a company that he, more than anyone else, had been responsible for creating. The Port Hope school play proved the breaking point for a rift that had been developing:

> It was less about the specific play and more about Robin not seeing his vision of what GCTC should be - a much further leftist organization doing

---

[20]   Author's interview with Arthur Milner.

agitprop full time on the stage, depression era theatre of the 1980s, always about the working man - and so to see us doing comedies or moving away from what he would want, that is a much more truly Marxist organization in terms of baseline aesthetic, I think that was the root of it. He could see that slipping away. But rather than being pleased to see what he and a few others had originated and what it was growing into, it infuriated him. It really did infuriate him. I can remember many discussions at different times and sharp little comments that he would make, and I can hear a few of them coming back now in the recesses of my brain, and it was always about programming: 'It's too soft. And where are we going?'[21]

Scott Duchesne, in his assessment of Robin and his cultural revolution, makes the following observation:

It was a step away from the kind of large-scale formative work (Mathews) felt the Great Canadian Theatre Company should be engaged in. Perhaps the shift even signalled a step towards the establishment of the company as a local "institution", with all the political and cultural obligations that label entails. This change in approach, however, enabled the company to nurture enough of an audience who could not imagine their lives without the GCTC as a voice for their particular concerns and aspirations. In contrast, the PTC (Penguin) and T2000 (Theatre 2000) were unable to develop the degree of audience loyalty the GCTC enjoyed by 1982. Both companies produced work that received critical acclaim, but they could not engender the degree of financial and audience support they needed to make the difficult transition to professional status, as well as to maintain the space and staff a professional company requires. The success of the GCTC, then, is partially based on the decision to shift its political leanings.[22]

Though Robin would hate the term and dismiss it as proof of a backslide into comprador capitalism, GCTC had a 'brand' that distinguished it from other Ottawa companies, including the NAC. GCTC was unabashedly left-wing and proudly, defiantly Canadian. In a small market, it stood out with what became, in the 80s and 90s, under the leadership of Milner and McDonald, a highly successful blend of entertainment and political theatre that still maintained a solid leftist bias. The irony is that Robin marked out the territory, determined

---

[21] Author's interview with Patrick McDonald.
[22] Duchesne, p 54.

the brand and then walked away from GCTC over an ideological dispute at the point when it was succeeding.

McDonald remembers Robin as someone who was "truly fearless" in defence of whatever his position was on any given subject, but most emphatically when defending his political worldview. But his and Milner's efforts to professionalize the company and grow its audience collided head-on with the Mathews worldview:

We have to remember the growing pains we had and the disagreements that we would have. Arthur and I, in particular, were charged with turning the company into a professional organization. But we were arguing with tenured professors. Arthur and I, as well as the people we employed, were just trying to make a living.

So we told them: 'You're okay financially, but you have to understand that at some point, you have to let us make the choices, and you're going to like some and you're going to dislike some.' And for the most part they liked most of our choices. But Robin being Robin, when he disliked the choice, you were going to know about it. That said, he and Esther's home was open to all the young folks who didn't have anybody around for Christmas, Thanksgiving, or Easter. And the wine would flow. The stories would flow, great stories. He was a wonderful raconteur. It was fascinating to be around him, but when you were in his eyeline as a target, it was never a pleasant day.[23]

What, then, is his legacy in the realm of Canadian theatre? A skeptic will point to a body of plays that served as polemical vehicles with characters who functioned as mouthpieces for Robin's worldview, were wooden, and lacked depth. Similarly, his plot lines were all too obviously and uncomfortably manipulative. It is unsurprising then that the plays have sunk into obscurity and are unlikely ever to be produced again. But that is a very narrow gauge by which to measure Robin Mathews. He was an extraordinary radical who inspired belief and a fierce determination in the right to own and articulate a Canadian narrative liberated from a British colonial past and current-day American imperialism. The cultural nationalism he inspired and nurtured created a space for others to flourish, among them Arthur Milner and Patrick McDonald, who went on to distinguished careers in Canadian theatre.

---

[23]   Author's interview with Patrick McDonald.

Milner was a GCTC playwright in residence from 1978 to 1991 and served as artistic director from 1991 to 1995 and again from 2005 to 2007. His impressive oeuvre includes plays engaging with challenging subjects, including *Facts* and *Getting to Room Temperature*. *Facts*[24] fictionalizes the real-life story of the unsolved killing of an archaeologist murdered in the West Bank in 1992. Premiered by GCTC in 2010, it is a provocative and disturbing exploration of the relationship between the two investigating police officers, one an Israeli, the other a Palestinian.

Facts has been produced numerous times to great critical acclaim and toured Israel and the West Bank in an Arabic translation. Its continuing relevance is underlined by the tragic and barbarous nature of the war in Gaza that began in 2023. *Getting to Room Temperature*, produced in 2016, examines the issues of aging and dying within the context of assisted suicides.

McDonald, who collaborated closely with Milner and directed many of his plays, was the GCTC's artistic director from 1981 to 1987. He left Ottawa to become the artistic director of Vancouver's Green Thumb Theatre, a position he held for more than twenty years, in that time directing 75 plays. Among the many distinguished playwrights whose plays McDonald has directed are George F. Walker, Joan MacLeod and Morris Panych. He is a multiple winner of the Jessie Richardson Theatre Award.

The actor, playwright and director Andrew Moodie[25] began his onstage career with the GCTC in 1987. His plays include *The Lady Smith*, which opened at Theatre Passe Muraille in 2000, *The Real McCoy* (2006) and *Toronto the Good* (2020), all of which were premiered by Toronto's Factory Theatre. Young playwrights who came of age in the 2000s were born and raised in Ottawa and had their first exposure to theatre with GCTC. Hannah Moscovitch,[26] whose work is produced across Canada and whose plays have won multiple awards, saw her play about the Warsaw Ghetto, *The Children's Republic*, premiered by GCTC in 2009. The Ottawa-born actor, playwright and television writer Rosa Labordé,[27] playwright in residence at Tarragon Theatre

[24] Arthur Milner, *Two Plays About Israel/Palestine*, iUniverse, 2012.
[25] Gaetan Charlebois and Anne Nothof, 'Moodie, Andrew', The Canadian Theatre Encyclopedia. https://www.canadiantheatre.com/dict.pl?term=Moodie%2C%20Andrew
[26] Anne Nothof, 'Moscovitz, Hannah', The Canadian Theatre Encyclopedia .https://www.canadiantheatre.com/dict.pl?term=Moscovitch%2C%20Hannah
[27] Miguel Máiquez, 'Rosa Labordé, the refreshing voice of Canadian Theatre', Lattin Magazine December 12, 2017. https://lattin.ca/2017/12/12/rosa-laborde-refreshing-voice-canadian-theatre/

and Aluna Theatre, credits GCTC[28] with supporting and developing her black comedy *Two Wolves*, which the company premiered in 2013. Morwyn Brebner[29] was born in Wales and grew up in Ottawa next door to Arthur Milner.

Milner's daughter and Brebner became, and remain, close friends. Brebner's first play, *Music for Contortionist*, premiered at Tarragon in 2000, and she has gone on to enjoy a career creating and writing several television series. While their careers have flourished in different ways, what marks them all is a commitment to thorny topics that are socially relevant and have a leftist perspective.

Critics, too, have come of age. No more are there questions about whether or not Canadian plays are culturally relevant or deserve to be staged. It is taken for granted and has been for many years that they are embedded in Canada's cultural landscape. The cultural nationalism that GCTC brought to the fore in the nation's capital and that raised the hackles of so many critics may, 50 years on, seem quaintly anachronistic, when in fact, it is a measure of a great victory, one that Robin was instrumental in helping to realize. His is a legacy to be marked and recognized. How very Canadian of us that we have allowed him to slip from sight without acknowledging how profound his contribution to Canadian theatre and culture has been.

Works Cited

Ascah, Adrienne. "Five Questions with Rosa Laborde', *Ottawa Sun*, June 2, 2013. https://ottawasun.com/2013/06/02/five-questions-with-rosa-laborde.

Benson, Eugene and L.W. Conolly. *The Oxford Companion to Canadian Theatre*, Oxford University Press, 1989.

Charlebois, Gaetan. 'Factory Theatre'. The Canadian Theatre Encyclopedia, Athabasca University Press. https://www.canadiantheatre.com/dict.pl?term=Factory%20Theatre

Duchesne, Scott. "'Fitful Excellence": The Great Canadian Theatre Company and English-Speaking Theatre in Ottawa, 1975-1983', PhD dissertation, University of Toronto, 2004.

---

[28]   Adrienne Ascah, 'Five Questions with Rosa Laborde', Ottawa Sun, June 2, 2013. https://ottawasun.com/2013/06/02/five-questions-with-rosa-laborde

[29]   Anne Nothof, 'Brebner, Morwyn', The Canadian Theatre Encyclopedia. https://www.canadiantheatre.com/dict.pl?term=Brebner%2C%20Morwyn

Garebian, Keith and Urjo Kareda. 'Tarragon Theatre', The Canadian Theatre Encyclopedia, Athabasca University Press, September 3, 2008. https://www.thecanadianencyclopedia.ca/en/article/tarragon-theatre

Law, Bill. Unpublished interview with Arthur Milner, November 15, 2023.

Law, Bill. Unpublished interview with Patrick McDonald, December 6, 2023.

LW Conolly Theatre Archives, University of Guelph Library. https://www.lib.uoguelph.ca/archives/our-collections/lw-conolly-theatre-archives/great-canadian-theatre-company/

Máiquez, Miguel. 'Rosa Labordé, the refreshing voice of Canadian Theatre', Lattin Magazine December 12, 2017. https://lattin.ca/2017/12/12/rosa-laborde-refreshing-voice-canadian-theatre/

Mathews, Robin and James Steele, editors. *The Fight for Canadian Universities*, New Press, 1969.

Milner, Arthur. *Two Plays About Israel/Palestine*, iUniverse, 2012.

Noonan, James. 'The National Arts Centre: Fifteen Years at Play', 1985 Theatre Research in Canada v6 n1 (198501): 56-81. https://journals.lib.unb.ca/index.php/tric/article/view/7430/8489

Nothof, Anne. The Canadian Theatre Encyclopedia, Athabasca University Press. https://www.canadiantheatre.com/dict.pl

Novick, Julius. 'Ecstasy: The Indian's Agony' The New York Times May 13, 1973. https://www.nytimes.com/1973/05/13/archives/ecstasy-the-indians-agony-theater-in-washington-dc.html

Rochdale College. https://en.wikipedia.org/wiki/Rochdale_College#:~:text=According%20to%20the%20CBC%20Archives,the%20beginning%20of%20the%20end.

ON BEING A WRITER: AN APPRECIATION OF ROBIN MATHEWS' CREATIVE WORK

By Misao Dean

B y the time of his death Robin Mathews had published ten poetry books, as well as one collection of short stories and numerous uncollected pieces. He also wrote plays for the Great Canadian Theatre Company, both as a single author (*Selkirk*, *A Woman is Dying*, *For Love Quebec*), and as a collaborator. This should be enough to be considered a substantial contribution to Canlit, but this is not how he is remembered; his political activism on the Canadian question in academia, his interventions as a literary critic and his reputation as a controversialist have completely overshadowed his creative writing. Yet in the Robin Mathews fonds at Library and Archives Canada is a piece of juvenilia that throws a surprising light on his career. It's a multipage typed MS, on foxed newsprint paper, called "On being a writer." Dated 1956, when the writer was 26, it reiterates various romantic stereotypes of the writer's life, including asserting that being a writer is a calling, a drive that is undeniable, to produce writing and to have it read, to "keep alive a persistent spirit" (5). It suggests that he thought of himself as a writer first, not a professor or an activist, a writer defined by all the clichés of inspiration and sensitivity. And the papers bear this out: Mathews' juvenilia aren't full of callow Marxist political analyses, but Romantic depictions of the writer as a singer, a voice, a craftsman, a vehicle for joy, beauty, and human frailty. This is a surprise, considering how bitter and caustic much of his creative writing seems, in hindsight.

Writer was far from a predicable profession for Mathews, who described himself as coming from genteel poverty on the outskirts of an isolated mill town. In an MS short story, "The Poverty Flower," the narrator, the younger son of the "Middleton" family,[1] describes growing up in Shacktown on the edge of a small community in BC, living a poverty-stricken existence while his

---

[1]   Mathews' full name was "Robin Daniel Middleton Mathews."

father worked as a part-time music teacher throughout the 1930s and 1940s. For this family, the narrator claims, the Depression didn't end until 1948; he describes siblings with only one pair of shoes, one set of clothes, and little in the way of food beyond bare subsistence. The parents are the heroes of the story. The narrator remains unaware that his family is poor until they are visited by well-off relatives who refuse the hospitality of the family home, described as a primitive shack surrounded not by marigolds or petunias but by the "poverty flower," Dame's Rocket (also known as wild phlox). The details of this story are clearly autobiographical: they express a deep shame and self-consciousness about being perceived as poor, and admiration for older brothers in labouring jobs and fighting overseas in World War II.

"On being a writer" was Mathews' mission statement, the wide-eyed but committed response of a small-town outcast to the intellectual and artistic world he met when he left home, first for an undergraduate degree at UBC, then for graduate studies at University of Ohio and University of Toronto.

Mathews' early books, *The Plink Savoir* (1962) and *Plus Ça Change* (1964),[2] show how he lived his mission to be a writer. His early work shows the strong influence of the modernist authors he was studying and teaching, with a focus on aesthetics and technique. From the first two stanzas of "Song" from *Plus Ça Change*:

> You whom I love,
> Lay your head down.
> Branches on branches
> Rustle and cringe.
> Willows make leaving sounds,
> Geese fly to Southward;
> Winter is crying
> Over the plain.
> . . .
> Faithful beloved,
> Lay your head down. (ll.1-8, 15-16)

The form, as well as the elegiac tone of address to the beloved, is clearly influenced by Auden's famous lyric, "Lullaby" (Lay your sleeping head), though "Song" uses two beats per line as opposed to Auden's four. Mathews

---

[2]   These books self-published in Edmonton continue to be rare. I consulted them in the Special Collections room at the MacPherson Library at University of Victoria.

fills the poem with imagery and vocabulary from nineteenth-century Canadian landscape poetry (soughing of waters, rustle and cringe, geese flying south) rather than Auden's faithlessness and erotic ennui. Like Auden's poem, Mathews' "Song" evokes the passage of time and the inevitability of mortality, but it does so through the imagery of a prairie fall and winter. Another example of his early work is the title poem of Mathews' first book, "The Plink Savoir." The poem celebrates the sounds of words by representing the playing of a samisen and a pipe:

Plink!
with your plectrum
pluck
at the samisen
golden-skinned Orpheus
sloe-eyed inciter
plink!
plink
Sloe-eyed inciter
or
careless lover
caparisoned in jangle
whistle and shake
make

shoeeshoee (ll. 1-15)

These three stanzas are a celebration of sound (assonance, onomatopoeia) in arbitrary short lines; they recall the modernist's fetishization of "the Orient" and the value of art. Many poems from *The Plink Savoir* evoke modernists like Dylan Thomas ("Night Dive") or Wallace Stevens ("Dilemma: Roses and Splinters of Sun") or Theodore Roethke ("Villanelle") but to say so is really to say nothing interesting: these poems demonstrate that Mathews, as a young man, was well read in canonical British and American authors, and extraordinarily skilled at absorbing both technique and tone from his reading. These are the elements of his work that his academic mentors probably saw: he was motivated, perceptive, hard-working, and sensitive to literary nuance. As influences, he tended to favour poets who, like him, came from a working-class background and celebrated the act of artistic creation as representing the best of humanity. And, of course, in each of these poems, he adapts the voices he emulates to convey imagery more familiar to a Canadian reader.

"A Narrative of Lilac, Naked by the Sea" from *Plus Ça Change*, rejects European imagery as inappropriate to the coastal Canadian setting of the poem:

> An old community
> Of oriental royalty in cuneiform pagodas
> Would only clutter up
> This Western shore.
> Imported majesty is all illusion,
> Make-believe,
> A managed disenchantment in this brackish atmosphere.
> The nightingale, remember, fades at evening into forests
> Far from these. Here, the mind is broken
> By the hoarse, complaining seagull cry. (ll.14-23)

The modernist "Oriental" pagoda, and the nightingale, fetish of the Romantic poets, are here rejected in favour of "nakedness." The poem declares that in the coastal setting, reality itself sums up "all that myth can concentrate or history relate" (l.39). These poems, derivative as they may be, give a sense of what Mathews' future work would be like.

An evolution toward a more direct and political voice seems to have taken place in poems published after Mathews and his wife Esther had lived in Europe from 1966-68. The couple were in Paris during the student uprising in the spring of 1968. They witnessed the million-strong student protests and the general strike that encompassed a third of the workforce, which forced Charles De Gaulle to flee the country and led to violent police crackdowns. The protestors targeted consumerism, American imperialism, and capitalism, as well as repressive traditional institutions, while the workers, eschewing their union leadership, struck for various goals ranging from better pay to control of the means of production. These protests famously had a huge effect on the generation of French intellectuals who lived through them, such as Foucault, Barthes, and Derrida, and many have written about the ferment of ideas and discussions relating to the relationship between the arts and politics that they led to. This was not the "New Left" of downtown Toronto, dominated by draft dodgers and poisoned by drug dealers,[3] but an entire society in flux. Mathews

---

[3] This is the way he characterized the Toronto members of the New Left in the poem, "Toronto: The Revolutionaries" in *Air* 7.

The failure of Toronto New Left projects like Rochdale College has been attributed by participants to organized criminal drug dealers.

was fluent in French, and he and Esther collected pamphlets, posters and ephemera from the protests (later donated to Simon Fraser University). When Mathews returned to Canada for a teaching position at Carleton, his poetry had achieved a distinctive, colloquial voice and a more direct political mission.

A comparison of *The Plink Savoir* and *Plus Ca Change* to the books that came later show a significant change in poetic voice. In "Valentine's Day: 1970," one of the poems collected in a special issue of *Air 7* (and later republished in *Language of Fire*)[4], Mathews contrasts the tone of Ottawa politics to his new idea of authentic engagement:

> It is easy to go to the theatre here,
> Or bend over a martini glass
> With old friends by a crackling fire
> Talking of pollution or separatism.
>
> There seems to be no sacrifice in it
> The heart seems all but dead
> The gossip is all of cabinet shuffles,
> And is, in a way, always true. (ll.9-16)

The poem contrasts the cozy conversation of Ottawa politicians and civil servants to the sacrifice and heart-forward engagement of the student protests around the world in 1968, and finds Ottawa "like a very long night . . . a very long death" (ll.17-18). The contrast between Paris in 1968 and Ottawa 18 months later was stark.

Mathews claimed to come from the working class because he did, and throughout his career, his poems remained conscious of his privilege in relation to those he grew up with. Before he left Canada in 1966, he was already an activist: he was arrested in October of 1963 for protesting the election of William Hawrelak as Mayor of Edmonton, a man who had previously been removed from office for "gross misconduct"[5] in business deals he negotiated with the city while

---

4   *Air 7* and *The Geography of Revolution* were both poor quality publications (newsprint paper, saddle stich binding) and had very limited circulation. When Mathews created his first substantial collection, *Language of Fire*, for Steel Rail Publishing, he selected poems from both collections as well as new work. Some poems discussed as appearing in *Language of Fire* first appeared in *Air 7* or in *Geography of Revolution* also appeared in *Language of Fire* or even later collections. A fuller discussion of Mathews work would have to include careful investigation to determine the publication history of each of these poems.

5   Daniel Ross, "Municipal Conflicts of interest in Canada, Old and New." *Active History* December 4, 2012. https://activehistory.ca/blog/2012/12/04/municipal-conflicts-of-interest-in-canada-old-and-new/

in office. But Mathews' politics were expressed in his early poetry in conventional ways, subordinated to modernist aesthetics that declared poetry to be "above" politics and that, as the U.S. poet Archibald MacLeish put it in a much-quoted adage, the "poem should not mean, but be." After his trip to France, where he witnessed a huge majority protesting American imperialism and engaged in discussions about the politics of literature, he began to write political satire and use direct address in his poetry, naming the names of politicians and political figures he condemned in direct violation of modernist aesthetics.

A good example of this new voice is the poem "I am told by A.J.M. Smith" from *Air 7*, in which the poet addresses the influential editor who, in his introduction to *The Book of Canadian Poetry*,[6] condemned the "native" voice in Canadian poetry and lauded the "cosmopolitan" poets influenced by international modernism:

I am told by A.J.M. Smith
(U.S. citizen since 1935)
That I should feel as he does
Which is like Yeats and Eliot and Ezra Pound.
But I feel like me.
I feel autumn uneasiness.
I hurt at the world outside
Going from colour all into night.
I suppose facing winter isn't easy,
The little dying,
The long dark,
Described in white.
It's partly that—
My autumn uneasiness.
But it's also thinking of all the Smiths
Who couldn't survive here,
And died *there*, long ago,
Rotting slowly,
In another man's country. (ll.1-19)

Here, the speaker refers to the enemy by name, accusing Smith personally of exhibiting the colonial cringe, while at the same time identifying him as a

---

[6]   A.J. M. Smith ed. *The Book of Canadian Poetry: A Critical and Historical Anthology*. A review by Coleman Rosenberger, "On Canadian Poetry," published in *Poetry* describes the categories of "Native" and "Cosmopolitan" as Smith uses them.

figure symbolic of "all the Smiths" who believed that U.S. citizenship would cure them of the "otherness" of being Canadian, and thus (perhaps) destroyed their true authentic selves. The speaker identifies himself as incurably Canadian by means of affect: *he feels* the "autumn uneasiness" at the anticipation of winter often expressed by Canadian landscape poets, and an attitude to seasonal change that is specific to our part of the world. The speaking voice is colloquial: rhythmic without regular metre, evocative without using unusual vocabulary or metaphor. The collection published in *Air 7* includes poems directly addressed to Smith, to the Prime Minister, to individual members of government, to fellow poets, artists, and professors, accusing them of triviality, colonialism, naivety, and complicity, poems whose defiance of modernist and post-modernist definitions of poetic disinterestedness would result in Mathews being seen primarily as a political activist, not a writer.

Mathews' return to Canada in 1968 also heralded the beginnings of the work he would become known for, the Canadianization of universities and his deep involvement in the struggle against U.S. imperialism. The beginnings of this era of what academics often refer to as "70s nationalism," was partly the result of worldwide anti-colonial activism of the 1960s, coinciding with the wave of (government sponsored) national celebrations that took place during the Canadian Centennial year. At the same time, Mathews became a member of "The Waffle," the radical wing of the NDP party, who had challenged David Lewis for the leadership of the Federal NDP and won a third of the vote.[7] Robin Mathews took these struggles to his workplace and advocated for the teaching of Canadian literature in Canadian universities, arguing not just for more books, teachers and scholarship but also that these goals could not be met without confronting the overwhelming dominance of foreign-born and trained scholars in Canadian universities.[8] As late as 2006, Steele and Mathews wrote: "What remained an outstanding practical question in the seventies was whether or not a Canadianization of the curriculum would or could ever occur in the presence of the many recently appointed scholars from abroad" (492-3).

Mathews spent the early 70s talking about the Canadianization of the universities, giving speeches during the school year at "Teach-ins" and other events across the country, often sponsored by teachers' associations and

---

[7]   See Cormier.

[8]   See Misao Dean, "Canadianization, Colonialism, and Decolonization: Investigating the Legacy of 'Seventies Nationalism' in the Robin Mathews Fonds," And Mathews and Steele, eds. *The Struggle for Canadian Universities*.

student societies critical of the education they were receiving.[9] He spoke about curriculum and hiring practices, but also about the relationship between Canada and Quebec, especially in context of the 1970 "Quebec crisis," which saw public figures kidnapped and murdered by the Front de la Liberation du Quebec, and the imposition of the War Measures Act restricting public speech and protest. And many of these speeches ended with a poem, "Death and Revolution,"[10] that appears as the last poem in the first section of his poetry collection *Language of Fire* (1976). In doing so, he allied himself with well-known Quebecers such as Michele Lalonde, whose poem "Speak White" was an important rallying cry for the *Independantiste* movement, and foreshadowed those of the 2011-12 "occupy" movement who made the public reading of political poetry central to their community building efforts.[11]

"Death and Revolution" was typical of the overtly "political" poetry that Mathews published in this period. For example, in "I am Told by AJ M. Smith," "Death and Revolution" contrasts what "they" tell Canadians about themselves with what the speaker feels when he investigates Canadians. While "they" say Canadians are only interested in possessing consumer goods, "comfort/ and the material lie" (ll.10-11), he sees something else in Canadians: "eyes full of darkness/Like the black, high moment of night/Just before the beginning of the coming day" (ll.17-19), and "all around them/At their roots/Green shoots/ Reaching up into the sharp air/Like the flames of revolution" (ll.28-32). Numerous poems echo this structure of "they" vs us: "Banff," which describes "ugly American" tourists in the park; "The Yankee Imperialists," which describes the entitled way that expatriate activists in Canada put themselves at the centre of political organizing; and "The liberal academics" which accuses his colleagues of teaching students to be "deft, articulate spokesmen/ for whatever present tyranny demands" (l.34). These are the poems that most often provoked the ire of critics, and even of allies; with their violent metaphors and blustering accusations, likening U.S. sentimentality to pus and liberal academics to "scavengers on the rubbish heaps of Power" (l.15), they resisted aesthetic readings, and accused and repelled the very people most likely to read them.

---

[9] See Cormier, 19-55. See also records of these speeches in LAC Robin Mathews fonds, MG 31 D190 Vol 10.

[10] Many of the MS speeches in in LAC Robin Mathews fonds, MG 31 D190 Vol 10 end with the notation "Death and Revolution," or "poem."

[11] Stephen Collis has written extensively on the use of poetry by the Vancouver "Occupy" group and other contemporary protests. See for example "Poetry in Protest." For Michele Lalonde, see the article "Michele Lalonde," in *The Canadian Encyclopedia*.

In a self-authored biography written (in the third person) in this period, Mathews gave his own spin on the change in his poetic voice: "Although his earlier poems tend to be more conventional and are often lyrical, by 1965, his political attitudes become dominant and shape a colloquial and witty style — a much freer form." He defended his polemics, saying "some may question the validity of the political attitudes, the poetic idiom is entirely appropriate for the emotional commitment of the artist" (Biography, 2). He rallied support for his style of direct address by asking his friend Milton Acorn (with whom he collaborated in the founding of Steel Rail Publishing in the mid-1970s) to write an introduction to *Language of Fire*. The new introduction (which replaced a draft introduction,[12] which still exists in the Archives) defended the political role of poetry, declaring that historical English poets like Milton propagandized for the cause of the Roundheads and that, indeed, poetry is "the best of propaganda because it ferociously states an irrefutable truth" (ix). Mathews himself was less categorical, claiming only that while "the poems do not offer solutions, they point out the fallacies and hypocrisies and compel the reader to think" (Biography p. 2).

This new poetic voice, while colloquial and even slangy, clung to inherited forms long after end-rhyme and regular metre had been rejected by the majority of his peers. "The Ballad of Peter Trudeau," from *Language of Fire*, is an accusation against the then current Prime Minister of collaboration with U.S. imperialism, written in regular four beat iambic couplets with a comic use of end rhyme to undercut the seriousness of what he says. "Peter Trudeau" doesn't care how he makes us "Safe to be used by the USA/Safe to be sold in the Liberal way" (ll.15-16).

As he flicks his rose and hums "tra la"
And he sets our troops on the Quebecois. (ll.19-20)

The poem is full of conspicuous winks to those in the know, and witty rhymes that evoke the public image of the now historical Prime Minister Pierre Trudeau and his trademark boutonniere. It uses swinging rhythm, and the jaunty rhyme of "tra-la" with Quebecois to critique the implementation of the War Measures Act. Trudeau is "The lover, the dilettante, swimmer and Pet,/ Canada's male Marie Antoinette" (ll.33-34); the language of "The Ballad of Peter Trudeau" is sarcastic and personal, a reminder of the eighteenth-century

---

[12] This draft introduction is titled "Growing Free: Poems of love and liberation (introduction)." "Growing Free" was previously considered as a title for *Language of Fire*.

tradition of witty satire in rhyming couplets by writers like Alexander Pope or John Dryden. More examples of this kind of poem appear in *The Death of Socialism* (1995). "The Joe Clark Song" (ironically "to be sung to the tune of Joe Hill") attacks Joe Clark for passivity in the face of U.S. foreign policy in Central America:

> "From Washington we get our news.
> They tell us what to think.
> They say the folk along the Gulf
> Aren't human and they stink.
> They're Commies, and they stink."

> "But that's not true, you know it too,
> So fight it Joe," says I.
> "They've bought me heart and soul," says he,
> "I've joined the Yankee lie."(ll.21-27)

Satire, of course, depends on its effect on a sense of moral outrage shared by author and reader; and not only were few readers prepared to accept this simplistic judgement of Pierre Trudeau or Joe Clark at the time, but in hindsight, the targets seem mistaken. After all, in the intervening years, the neo-liberalism of the new Conservative party has been the bigger threat to both free speech and Canadian economic independence, despite their current claim to be the defenders of all things national. The reason satire became less popular in contemporary writing was that it depended on an ideological and moral consensus about what was worth attacking and how, and this consensus was less and less available in the late 20th and 21st centuries. A.M. Klein discovered this in 1944 when he wrote *The Hitleriad*,19, one of his least successful books; in 1944, even Hitler wasn't someone Canadians could all agree on. In contrast, George Bowering's satiric novels, such as *A Short Sad Book* (1977) and *Burning Water* (1980), laid themselves open to a variety of interpretations and so were more easily seen as post-modernist irony, with indeterminate meaning, and no obvious "message." The energy and jokiness of Mathews' satires could only be shared by true believers, who were (and continue to be) few on the ground among poetry readers.

Mathews' use of traditional techniques like formal satire, regular metre, and end rhyme was motivated by his belief that some kinds of experimental form were, in effect, a rejection of the humanist goals of poetry: of ideas in the broad sense of communal discourse, of the language of love, and the value of poetry to create social change. Instead, he saw most experimental poetry as merely "verse that offends no one but seems exciting" ("Growing free" 1); "typographical experiment, and tiny, personalist anguish, anything that shocks the senses without asking real questions" ("Growing Free" 1). In an article on poetics published in *CVII* in 1976, he rejected Frank Davey's idea that "tightly controlled, formalistic and elegant poetry" ("Poetics" 4) necessarily "shared formal assumptions with a company directorship" and cited the example of Archibald Lampman's sonnet, "To a Millionaire," which despite its formal regularity attacks "exploitation and abuse of defenseless humanity" ("Poetics" 4). Experimental form and indeterminate meaning are not the way to oppose capitalism, he argued, and to the extent that experimental form made literature inaccessible to ordinary readers, it played into the hands of the powerful. His poetic response to Davey, the sonnet "To a Billionaire," written in the style of Lampman's poem, appeared in the collection *The Death of Socialism*.

Mathews' academic work provides the context for these choices—his articles identify a tradition of Canadian writing that was skeptical of modernist and post-modernist experiment, committed to accessibility, and skilled in using all the resources that poetry offered. In an unpublished introduction to *Language of Fire*, he lays out this tradition: "Isabella Valancy Crawford, Archibald Lampman, F. R. Scott, Earle Birney, Dorothy Livesay, Alden Nowlan, Milton Acorn" ("Growing Free" 3). All of these poets made use, to a greater or lesser extent, of the strategies of traditional poetry: symbolism, allegory, rhyme, metre, the counted line, inherited forms like sonnets, villanelles, satires, and narrative poems, and none found the form impeded their ability to attack capitalism or celebrate working-class people. Mathews was consciously writing himself into that tradition and rejecting the contemporary poets who "want form to take precedence over what's said. So they call for revolutionary form. But there's only revolutionary content" ("Growing Free" 2). Revolutionary content explicitly promoted a hard-left idea of revolution: collective action forcing political and economic change for the betterment of working people, the nationalization of industry for the public good, and the overthrow of the classes by the masses. Social revolution—the destruction of the nuclear family, rejection of collective identities, the celebration of globalism, and of opportunities offered by new technologies—didn't count, and sentimental representations of suffering without naming and shaming the oppressors weren't good enough. For Mathews, revolutionary content required the poet to embrace his social positioning in even the most lyrical writing, to reject solipsism and confessional writing, and instead to reach out to fellow humans in solidarity even in their most private moments.

Some of the most affecting and memorable poems from *Language of Fire* and the subsequent books (*The Beginning of Wisdom* (1978), and *The Death of Socialism* (1995) eschew the more public voice of satire and invective for a more private tone, and increasingly, the themes of death and mortality. "Learning to Laugh and Cry" describes an elderly poet who dances beneath an apple tree in celebration of Beauty, shaking loose the remaining apples that "fall without note,/becoming earth as they touch it" (ll.26-27). "Springsong" strikes the exact opposite note, celebrating the feeling of youth and energy by describing his eleven-year-old son. But the poems that are perhaps the most successful in the book join the private lyric voice to its public significance. "Pre-history lesson," the final poem in *Language of Fire*, laments the signs of social dissolution and comments that young people have lost trust in public culture, "Crouching inside themselves like lithe tigers."

"You tell us about poetry and love, mister,
But the world makes contracts with the blades of blunt knives,
Writing, always, into somebody's flesh."(ll.13, 15-17)

The poet replies, "poems are swords/ or firebrands to burn down castles with,/ or blades of grass in the sun/where the oppressed find roads to liberation . . . poems are all those things,/and love is revolution" ll.26-29,31-32). The imagery of capitalism as cut into the skin with the "blades of blunt knives," creates a central contrast with the "blades of grass" that line the road to love and revolution. "Pre-history lesson" outlives its historical moment in a way that the satires can't. "Even running hard to get the golden prize" from *The Death of Socialism* turns the cliché of life as a race into something different by questioning what the goal is supposed to be, and concluding that the poet runs to experience "life/that surges from the dark earth/and will not be stayed" (ll.61-63). These poems, like "And when the sun came out," "A Rebours," and "The Geography of Revolution," will still resonate with readers who don't remember the specifics of the Trudeau regime or the names of specific opportunistic cabinet ministers.

For a fan of contemporary poetry, the experience of reading these books was mixed. Mathews' close friend Rob McDougall wrote in a letter of thanks for a copy of *Language of Fire*: "I find it a lonely and in some ways wistful book, its gentle and honest subtitle [*Poems of Love and Struggle*] fitting its essence better than the red-faced *Language of Fire*. I do not much like Milton Acorn's Introduction, with its blustering argument about propaganda and poetry and its swaggering claims for a people's poetry. And it is when you follow Acorn in this retreat (it can only be called that) to dogmatism that you are least convincing as a poet. It will not surprise you that I like best the poems which generate their own truth and are not dependent on a falsework of ideology to shore them up . . . Your wit, which has a twinkle in it, saves you many a time from a fearful fall, and some of the longer pieces, like the Bethune poem, are very impressive." (McDougall to Mathews 23 Aug 1976). McDougall read the lyrics as the centre of the book, with their honesty and expressiveness, the more evocative political poems next in importance; he dismissed they/ us poems and the accusatory addresses to individuals. It was a generous and perceptive assessment, like its author.

Language of Fire also included a short story: "The biggest bridge in the world," which represented the feelings of alienation of an American engineer working on a megaproject in northern Canada. Like many characters in Mathews' stories (the professor in "Kingsmere" comes to mind), the engineer is unable to distinguish between his desire for acceptance and his desire for domination; he feels isolated and out of his depth, and the superficial resemblance between his own culture and that of his workers only adds to his confusion. His eventual expression of anger and contempt has as much to do with his feeling of frustrated desire as with any political analysis of his position in a capitalist hierarchy. But despite this interesting plot, "The biggest bridge in the world" fails for the reason that many Mathews stories fail: technique. The conversations are stilted; "no one talks like that!" wrote reviewer Robin Endres in *Canadian Literature* (Endres 161). And the narrative voice always sounds the same. Like the poems, the stories frequently wear a "message" on their sleeve, a technique that many readers found frustrating. Realist fiction is supposed to dramatize, not preach. Robin Endres wrote: "just when I'm warming up to a story he will start bending it in some moralistic, self-righteous way to suit his ideological position. Even when the position has nothing to do with nationalist politics, I am suspicious, I feel he's trying to get me to think in a certain way" (161). When the story collection *Blood Ties*[13] appeared in 1984, critics praised "His own son," which had appeared previously in *Saturday Night*, for its emotional complexity and its unresolved ending, but dismissed many of the stories as didactic and stiff.

---

[13]   Robin Endres, "In Italics" (Rev. of Blood Ties).

By the time *Blood Ties* appeared, many of the collective projects that Mathews was involved in founding during the 1970s – Steel Rail publishing, The Great Canadian Theatre Company, and the Association for Canadian and Quebec Literatures – were struggling not only for funding but for direction. The "New Left" that had inspired the nationalist movement had been defeated: the Waffle had been expelled from the NDP party, following a motion crafted by the (recently canonized) Ed Broadbent. Members of the FLQ who had been jailed after the October Crisis were applying for parole, and running for office, repudiating their revolutionary pasts. The enemy no longer seemed to be the U.S. per se, and certainly not individual Americans working in Canada; left-wing and educated readers were interested in the rapid growth of neo-liberalism, the withdrawal of the federal government from funding social programs, the effects of the globalization of labour markets, the impact of new technologies on working people, the destruction of the environment, racism and homophobia, and Indigenous resurgence – all of these issues seemed pressing, and revolution seemed very far in the future.

A dispute, discussed in this collection by Bill Law in his essay "Great Canadian Theatre Company: in the Beginning," during the late seventies and early eighties over the direction of the Great Canadian Theatre Company illustrates the problems Mathews faced. Mathews had clashed with board members and with the artistic director Larry McDonald over the script of his play inspired by the FLQ crisis, *For Love Quebec*, in 1978. The play took the point of view of Quebecois separatists who had kidnapped a politician, and dramatized their panic, fear, and ideological quarreling, but also lauded their commitment and their goals. McDonald and director Bill Law wrote a long letter to Mathews declaring that while they understood the play was fiction, they wanted nothing to do with a play that suggested the real-life murder of Pierre Laporte by members of the FLQ had been justified (McDonald to Mathews, nd). Mathews characteristically replied passive-aggressively, suggesting that as director and artistic director, they were free to suggest rewrites. The play was staged, so presumably, the disagreement was resolved, but it heralded problems to come. As the GCTC had "professionalized," its collective decision-making structure was dropped, and board members and hired staff were uninterested in many of the plays Mathews wanted to produce, plays that like "For Love, Quebec," were so radical as to be practically guaranteed to lose money. While the theatre continued to promote Canadian plays and hire local actors and crew, they wanted to follow the interests of their union members and left-liberal supporters and dramatize issues that appealed to them. Mathews became the only voice arguing for the original vision of the company, staging plays that promoted hard-left ideas and were limited to Canadian topics and settings. It was a lonely place to be.[14]

Robin Endres characterized Mathews in the mid-eighties as a "Black fly (not a gadfly)": "We all know what he thinks; he's been on about it for years now, and is there anyone, left, centre or right, who actually agrees with his views on the national question? He is obsessed. It's annoying, but it's also what makes him interesting, as a thinker and as a writer" (160-61). Colleagues and supporters found him annoying as a plague of black flies, but had to admit, his work was never boring. His post-1980 non-fiction writing (including *Canadian Identity, Major Forces Shaping the Life of a People* (1988), *Treason of the Intellectuals* (1995), and many, many contributions to radical and online publications) carried on personalized disputes with academics and public figures he perceived as promoting (U.S.) liberal individualism at the expense of (Canadian) communitarian conservatism. Some of his later poems continue these battles, but many express a more vulnerable self, observant, loving, and playful. These are the poems I choose to remember. The portrait of his father in "On joining the Men's Movement" and his family in "The Poverty Flower"; the cheerful strangers in "The Day the Sun Came Out"; the distractions along the way in "Even Running Hard": "a rainbow trout in clear water/like a morning glory/moving to the surface with an explosion/opening a trumpet mouth/in perfect/silence" (ll.23-28). In "Japanese Plum Blossoms," a friend recovering from cancer wonders if her political commitment had contributed to her illness, and asks him to be more positive: "a person should try to be positive, should fight positively for the good" (ll.18-19). The speaker responds with a beautiful description of "the twigs of Japanese plum trees/ swollen with buds ready to burst into familiar,/ unimaginably beautiful blossoms" (36-38) But this "positivity" is really self-deception: "we can hardly seize even a single good instant/because we know all about plum blossoms rotting/in dark hollows,/ physical pain, broken beauty,/gods going out like sputtering candles" (ll.41-45). Yes. We do. At least, I do.

In the end, Robin Mathews worked like most of us to somehow remain true to his political principles and his analysis of the issues and problems in our society, and so, like most of us, he lived alienated from the majority of his

---

[14] Much of the above controversy is discussed in detail in Scott Kesi Duchesne, "Fitful Excellences": The Great Canadian Theatre Company and English-speaking Ottawa Theatre, 1975-1983."

own society. As a result, some of his creative work seems increasingly offensive and wrong-headed as time goes by, and he was rarely praised as a poet, despite his manifest strengths and his occasional brilliance. What happened to that ambitious, lyrical young man who wrote "On being a writer"? Are all activists doomed to become cranky, obsessive, and bitter, as the causes they hold close are overshadowed by others, and their beliefs distorted and misunderstood by subsequent generations? Is left political commitment self-sabotage? Robin made me ask these questions, and I'm better for it. Canadian writing has lost an important perspective, if one that was sometimes as annoying as a blackfly.

Works Cited

Auden, William H. "Lyric 33." W.H. Auden *Selected Poems* ed. Edward Mendelson. Random House, 1979. Pp. 50-51

Bowering, George. *A Short Sad Book*. Talonbooks, 1977.

~ *Burning Water*, General Publishing, 1980.

Collis, Stephen. "Poetry in Protest," *On Contemporary Practice* https://oncontemporarypractice.squarespace.com/pdf-archive .

Dean, Misao. "Canadianization, Colonialism, and Decolonization: Investigating the Legacy of 'Seventies Nationalism' in the Robin Mathews Fonds." *Studies in Canadian Literature*, vol. 41, no. 1, 2016, pp. 27-.

Duchesne, Scott Kesi. "Fitful Excellences": The Great Canadian Theatre Company and English-speaking Ottawa Theatre, 1975-1983" PhD dissertation 2004 University of Toronto.

Endres, Robin. "In Italics" (Rev. of *Blood Ties*). *Canadian Literature* No. 107 (1985) pp. 160-162.

Klein, A. M. *The Hitleriad, Collected works of A.M. Klein: the Poems Part 2 Original Poems 1937-1955.* ed. Zailig Pollock. University of Toronto Press, 1990 pp. 581-606.

McDonald, Larry and Bill Law to Robin Mathews, nd. MG31 D190n vol 41 file 41-12. Robin Mathews fonds, Library and Archives Canada.

McDougall, Robert to Mathews, 23 August 1976. MG 31 D190 Vol 1 file 1-12. Robin Mathews fonds, Library and Archives Canada.

Mathews, Robin. "A Narrative of Lilac, Naked by the Sea" *Plus Ça Change*. Self-published Edmonton 1964, p. 14.

~ "And when the sun came out," in *Language of Fire*. Steel Rail Publishing, 1976, p.111.

~ "A Rebours," in *Language of Fire*, Steel Rail Publishing, 1976, p. 68.

~ "Banff" in *Language of Fire*. Steel Rail Publishing, 1976, p. 37.

~ "Biography." Typescript. MG 31 D190 Vol 1 file 1-7. Robin Mathews fonds, Library and Archives Canada.

~ "Death and Revolution" in *Language of Fire*. Steel Rail Publishing, 1976, p. 49

~ "Dilemma: Roses and Splinters of Sun" *Plus Ça Change*. self published, Edmonton, 1964, p. 16

~ "Even running hard to get the golden prize" in *The Death of Socialism and other poems*. Voyageur Publishing, 1995, pp. 103-105.

~ "Growing Free: Poems of love and liberation (introduction)" Typescript. MG 31 D190 Vol 43 file 43-24. Robin Mathews fonds Library and Archives Canada.

~ "I am told By A.J.M. Smith" in *Air* 7, 1972, n.p.

~ "Japanese Plum Blossoms" in *The Death of Socialism and other poems*. Voyageur Publishing, 1995, pp. 50-53.

~ ""Learning to Laugh and Cry" in *The Death of Socialism and other poems*. Voyageur Publishing, 1995, p.95

~ "Night Dive" *The Plink Savoir*. Self-published. Edmonton, 1962, n.p.

~"On Joining the Men's Movement" in *The Death of Socialism and other poems*. Voyageur Publishing 1995, pp. 80-83.

~ "Pre-history lesson," in *Language of Fire*. Steel Rail Publishing, 1976, p. 118.

~ "The Ballad of Peter Trudeau" in *Language of Fire*. Steel Rail Publishing, 1976, pp. 60-61.

~ "The Geography of Revolution," in *Language of Fire*. Steel Rail Publishing, 1976 pp. 42-47.

~ "The Joe Clark Song" in *The Death of Socialism and other poems*. Voyageur Publishing, 1995 pp. 42-44.

~ "The liberal academics" in *Language of Fire*. Steel Rail Publishing, 1976 p. 62.

~ "The Plink Savoir" *The Plink Savoir*. Self-published, Edmonton, 1962. n.p.

~"The Poverty Flower" MS short story Robin Mathews Fonds LAC Robin Mathews fonds, MG 31 D190 Vol 11 file 11-28.

~ "The Yankee Imperialists" in *Language of Fire*. Steel Rail Publishing, 1976, p. 19.

~ "To a Billionaire" in *The Death of Socialism and other poems*. Voyageur Publishing, 1995, p. 20.

~ "Song" *Plus Ça Change.* Self-published, Edmonton, 1964. p. 11

~ "Springsong" in *Language of Fire* Steel Rail Publishing, 1976, p. 92.

~ "Valentines' Day, 1970" in *Air* 7, 1972 n.p.

~ "Villanelle" *Plus Ça Change,* self-published, Edmonton, 1964 P. 13

~"Poetics: The Struggle for Voice in Canada" Box MG D190 vol 9 File 9-27 typescript 9 pages. Robin Mathews fonds Library and Archives Canada.

Mathews, Robin and James Steele, eds. *The Struggle for Canadian Universities.* Toronto: New Press, 1969.

Rochon, Francois. "Michele Lalonde" *The CanadianEncyclopedia* https://www.thecanadianencyclopedia.ca/en/article/michele-lalonde.

Rosenberger, Coleman. "On Canadian Poetry." *Poetry,* Volume 63, Number 5, 1944, pp. 281–87.

Ross, Daniel. "Municipal Conflicts of interest in Canada, Old and New." *Active History* December 4, 2012. https://activehistory.ca/blog/2012/12/04/municipal-conflicts-of-interest-in-canada-old-and-new/

Smith A.J.M. ed. *The Book of Canadian Poetry: A Critical and Historical Anthology,* with an Introduction and Notes. University of Chicago Press, 1944.

Steele, James and Robin Mathews. "Canadianization Revisited: a comment on Cormier's 'The Canadianization Movement in Context.'" *The Canadian Journal of Sociology / Cahiers canadiens de sociologie* Volume 31, Number 4 (Autumn, 2006), pp. 491-508.

THE ROBIN MATHEWS PROJECT: KNOWING CANADA

By Susan Crean

I came to know Robin Mathews in the mid-seventies when the political Left was active and demonstrating in the streets. I was involved with the women's movement and participated in local actions, including the annual peace march. What was becoming obvious then was the presence of American pop culture in new forms — videocassettes and, ultimately, CDs — meaning television and radio were no longer the only outlets for mass media. This expansion was something that came with the branch plant economy and one that tended to replace local production with foreign content. The exchange is, and continues to be, the major downside to foreign ownership in Canada. One hot issue at the time was the role of Canada's home-grown cable companies, who were making large amounts of money distributing television signals to Canadian homes from U.S. border stations (like Buffalo) while contributing little, if anything, to the creation of Canadian culture. For this, they were disparagingly likened to "parking lot attendants."

The ensuing license hearing resulted in a CRTC requirement that cable companies make a community channel universally available. The new regulation existed for some time, but the concept did not make for watchable programming, though it was informative, especially concerning community activities. Predictably, it silently disappeared and became a marker of the familiar Canadian conundrum about what could (or should) have been. The overshadowing issue is who we are as a society. That issue did not disappear. Canadian broadcasting policy has always invited questions about who we are. And, in retrospect, what we might have been doing instead.

The real story then was not so much the Americans across the border or the pro-Americans here who only saw the cash in the exchange, but the cold shoulder given Canadian writing, film and visual arts by institutions like art museums, Canadian book publishing, and the performing arts. It was also evident in post-secondary and university curricula. Something Robin Mathews, as an English Literature professor at Carleton University, understood and was willing to write about. Much worse, he was willing to talk about it, too.

I spent a good deal of time in Ottawa during the seventies and eighties working freelance for the CBC and NFB. So, I spent time with Robin, his wife Esther and their family (Rosamund, Sabrina and Hrothgar), where the conversation often turned to Canadian culture. These were good times that included wonderful, freewheeling conversation and also the luxury of spending time with children. Indeed, knowing Robin prompted me to consider the Canadian content all around me and, by the same token, what Canadian material I had been introduced to in literature and history classes at school. Truth be told, in those thirteen years, it was next to nothing. I introduced myself to Canadian literature and art.

Back then, I was writing backgrounders for groups like the Canadian Conference of the Arts (CCA) and short pieces for community newspapers. Mathews was prolific; he wrote and talked about the issues, mesmerizing his students and encouraging others to join the struggle. He was an enthusiast, though never uncritical. Moreover, Robin took an interest in others, especially those travelling the same rocky, uphill road. The difference was that he listened — and then argued a lot.

Moreover, the issues he was charting were as novel as they were high-stakes. I'd worked with several people on papers examining cultural policy — academics, activists, bureaucrats and consultants — but I'd never met anyone like Robin, combining serious on-the-ground politics while wearing his heart on his sleeve. He was a silver-tongued poet, indeed. And few outside Ireland could argue with the clarity and conviction as Robin did. He gave freely to anyone who'd listen. A committed, pro-active writer, his day job teaching only made him more eloquent. He was shrewd and jovial but deadly serious in his determination to transform Canada by taking on the elites.

By the seventies, the arts in Canada were well-established in terms of production companies — and artists co-operatives had advanced a few individual artists, such as Margaret Atwood, Shirley Bear and Lillian Allen, who did indeed acquire national and occasionally international reputations. However, while the work of Canadian artists was becoming more widely available, and the cultural industries (filmmaking, music recording, book and magazine publishing) were established and reasonably stable, it was mainly due to the policies and funding from three levels of government in support of these enterprises. (And some private/individual donors, often including individual artists themselves, who were typically in the position of subsidizing the event.)

Yet, a good many of these organizations, particularly the older 'legacy' companies (the Canadian Opera Company, National Ballet, Toronto

Symphony Orchestra), were not much interested in original Canadian material, preferring to use non-Canadian work, importing British or American content. Some fields were unionized (acting, musical performance), which made a difference, while other fields were still evolving. In the seventies, visual artists set up Canadian Artists Representation/Front des Artistes Canadiens [CAR/ FAC] and moved to professionalize their relationship with public art galleries whose standard practice when exhibiting contemporary work was to pay everyone involved except the artists. (For a time, at the beginning, I worked as the organization's executive secretary.)

Robin was prolific; he wrote and talked about the issues with his students as well as colleagues and friends while always encouraging other freelance thinkers to join the struggle. He was an enthusiast, though never uncritical. And he took an interest in others, especially those travelling the same rocky, uphill trail. The difference was that he listened — and then argued a lot.

My study, commissioned by the Programme in Arts Administration at York University's Business School, first of all involved pulling together a list of professional arts organizations such as symphony orchestras, theatre, opera and dance companies, art galleries, and publishers across the country. The primary funding source for their activities was the fledgling Canada Council for the Arts. This operation had been funding the arts and artists since 1957, although the provinces were increasingly contributing. But not even the Canada Council had a comprehensive list. So, my first job was sleuthing one down. I consulted John Hobday at the Canadian Conference of the Arts and got access to his list. But as this was before computers, it meant a card index and Xerox machine. I then wrote to organizations across the country, asking about their programs, and heard back from most. However, somehow, I wasn't expecting the picture that actually emerged — which was the strange absence of Canadian work. Right across the disciplines, the content being presented and performed in all fields was imported. Be it the visual arts, filmmaking, music, theatre, or publishing, there seemed to be an operative disinclination to present the work of Canadians, especially the living ones. Moreover, there was little interest in addressing the underfunding of Canadian culture as a whole.

This neglect of Canadian art and artists translated into a sector that primarily existed as a cottage industry. Artists were paid last and paid least. This situation meant arts and culture as a whole existed like a kind of inverted pyramid, its peak displaying creators and their work, pointing straight into the ground. At the same time, the supporting substructure (now super-structure)

85

took precedence. This arrangement was valid even in the case of well-funded crown corporations and national institutions like the CBC and the NFB. Hence, the title of the report I wrote is: *Who's Afraid of Canadian Culture? Report of a Study of the Diffusion of the Performing Arts in Canada.*[1] It was 1973, and the study published was one of a kind, and in its way, radical. This is to say that few people in the arts at the time (think Canadian Opera Company or the Toronto Symphony Orchestra) had thought to take an interest in Canadian content.

In 1973, this set of results stood in sharp contrast to cultural policies at work in Quebec, where home-grown work was prioritized. The Quebec example was in itself galvanizing. I began writing short essays and joined the editorial collective of *This Magazine*, working with thinkers, unionists and activists like Mel Watkins, Madeleine Parent, Rosemary Sullivan, Laurell Ritchie, Rick Salutin and Danny Drache. And as several of us were active in the Women's movement, I started a column called "Female Complaints" and others were invited to write for it. (Timothy Findley was memorably the lone man to offer.) Like many others, I had become an activist, demonstrating, writing, speaking out and attending demonstrations addressing the dearth of Canadian content in the arts. Not all of us were from the post-war generation. There were elder activists in some abundance, and I watched individuals with years of experience — teachers, researchers, and lawyers — become activists by taking on extraordinary roles and causes. At the head of that line was Robin Mathews. Thinking about this history now puts me in mind of today's younger activists and groups like Extinction Rebellion, which has taken on climate change by disrupting ordinary life, for example, by occupying bridges. Halting daily life in the hope of prompting some sober second thoughts.

Actually, Robin's great gift as a teacher and an activist was his outspoken nature, for he didn't distinguish between the two roles he took in life — teacher and activist. What he was building, of course, was community. And what drew me to him was his uncompromising stance on Canadian content. The first time I saw him in action was at the annual meeting of the members of the Art Gallery of Ontario in the early seventies. I was there with a couple of activists, one being my partner Peter Wilson, an artist and member of the artists' union, CAR/FAC. You could say our presence was a class action in

---

[1] Crean, Susan, *Who's Afraid of Canadian Culture? Report of a Study of the Diffusion of the Performing Arts and Exhibiting Arts in Canada*, published by the Programme in Arts Administration, York University,1973.

both senses of the term 'class.' We were there as workers, not board members or funders. We wanted to address the issues of Canadian content and creators' rights. So, the main point for our being there was to make an intervention about the gallery's apparent disinterest in Canadian art. Indeed, it wasn't long before Robin was on his feet, talking about cultural imperialism and the role institutions like the AGO had in promoting American artists while keeping Canadian artists in the background. He finished by asking the AGO's director, William Withrow, how he could sleep at night given the gallery's recorded disinterest in and disrespect for Canadian art and artists. Withrow blanched, a few people gasped, others clapped, and the meeting continued.

Earlier in July 1972, the announcement of the appointment of Pennsylvania-born and educated Richard J. Wattenmaker as head curator of the Art Gallery of Ontario caused a group of demonstrators, named the Committee to Strengthen Culture "led by an individual dressed in an Uncle Sam costume, marched from Trinity Square at the University of Toronto, past the U.S. consulate, and headed straight to the AGO." [2] Jeffrey J. Cormier describes the scene in his book *The Canadianization Movement: Emergence, Survival and Success*: "Once there, four of the protesters entered the offices of the new curator and chained themselves to his desk. They had a letter for Wattenmaker to sign that stated: 'I have come to realize that my appointment as chief curator is detrimental to the people of Canada.' A month earlier, about 20 Canadian artists "tied themselves together with a rope in front of a Toronto art gallery in symbolic protest against the announcement that Wattenmaker has been given the job. They publicly read a letter to the gallery's director, William Withrow, demanding full disclosure of the process involved in Wattenmaker's appointment. There, Jim Brown, a member of the Canadian Liberation Movement, and Mathews' friend and ally, read a letter saying, "This is just a symptom of the disease Canadian culture is in. We've got to stop it here. We've got to reverse this decision." [3]

Canadian content as a concept and an issue was launched. It came up most regularly in those days concerning television and radio licenses and the Canadian Radio-Television Commission (CRTC), which granted them. But the issue pertained equally to book publishing, filmmaking, recorded music and the programmes of art galleries and museums. However, Canadian work

---

[2]   Cormier, Jeffrey. *The Canadianization Movement: Emergence, Survival, and Success*, University of Toronto Press, Toronto, 2004, p. 4.

[3]   Ibid, p. 4.

across the genres and media saw the light of day mostly because of small, independent organizations, not the large mainstream ones. The branch-plant system, coupled with foreign ownership, conspired to keep Canadian manufacturing on the margins in many fields — a situation which was, at first, more visible in textiles and car manufacturing than in the arts. But who even thought of artists and creators as workers, never mind the concept of the cultural industries back in the seventies? What was most significant was how this optic coincided with a surge of grass-roots activism inherited from the late sixties. Now, it was happening not only in the women's and peace movements but also in the trade unions. Creators who took pride in the collective accomplishment of workers in their field took to the streets. The targets were the large, multinational corporations and government policy. But also, local institutions, such as the Art Gallery of Ontario, called the police when artists turned up to demonstrate at the front entrance. A visible example of class warfare, if you like.

In short, the issue Robin was charting was as novel as it was high-stakes. I'd worked with a number of people on articles and papers to do with cultural policy — academics, activists, bureaucrats and consultants — but here was someone combining serious on-the-ground politics with his day-job teaching, meaning he was educating his students not only about history, what went before, but about what was to come, and their possible involvement in affecting the future.

The term "Canadian Content," invented at that time for political reasons, took some getting used to. But it alluded to something serious, which some described as the 'cultural inferiority' of Canadians — meaning the institutionalized disinterest in our past and, by implication, in our future — by the very institutions that should be most engaged with it. What we encountered then, and what changed things, was the organized political Left—organized in terms of street activism, as well as the union movement and lefties at large. Robin was part of the generation making waves. For what he was dealing with was Canada's infatuation with America. An old song, but nonetheless one that remains critical — and one he was good at answering.

Furthermore, it was becoming apparent that, given the way the media was developing, there was going to be a reckoning. There would be a demand for more content. And that's precisely what happened.

Yet the exercise in getting there meant taking Canada and Canadians seriously and, simultaneously, taking the arts and the institutions and running them seriously. The term' Canadian Content' took some getting used to, but as an issue, what it alluded to was far more challenging to define. That would be the ideology of those cultural institutions and their open disinterest in Canadian content. The very term, Canadian content, seemed to be a put-down of our interest in our country and our generation of creators.

What I encountered in those years and what changed everything was the organized political Left. Organized in terms of activism in the cultural sector, as well as the union movement and Lefties at large. So, the story here is not only about political activism. More accurately, it is about the culture itself and how left-wing nationalism changed the country and Canadian culture. Robin Mathews put Canadian content on the map and made a public issue of it, pissing off the establishment on behalf of us all. In short, by encouraging a level of defiance in our generation, we effectively put home-grown culture on the national agenda.

Three years after the release of my study, which I titled *Who's Afraid of Canadian Culture: Report of a Study of the Diffusion of the Performing and Exhibiting Arts in Canada*," General Publishing brought out a book with the same title and the banner headline: "The Survival of Canadian Culture and the Canadian Nation is in Danger. But there is a way to save us." Decorated with a fading maple leaf for any readers who might miss the message, I see it today as a tribute to Robin, whose name I featured in the list of those who assisted in its conception.

Works Cited

Cormier, Jeffrey. The Canadianization Movement: Emergence, Survival, and Success. University of Toronto Press, Toronto, 2004.

Crean, Susan. *Who's Afraid of Canadian Culture: Report of the Diffusion of the Performing and Exhibiting Arts in Canada*. York University, Toronto, May, 1973.

Crean, S.M. *Who's Afraid of Canadian Culture*. General Publishing, Toronto, 1976.

ROBIN MATHEWS:
FOR INDEPENDENCE AND SOCIALISM

By Errol Sharpe

Introduction

In 1972 the author and other members of the Canadian Liberation Movement (CLM), a left nationalist movement advocating not just for independence from the U.S. but for a socialist Canada, gathered in Robin and Esther Mathews' basement to make picket signs to be used the next day in a demonstration to protest President Richard Nixon's April 14 visit to Ottawa. The basement activity itself was filmed by the CBC and broadcast nationally. It is a testament to Mathews' political sympathies that he would invite CLM activists to his basement, where their activity was being recorded by the CBC, rather than the Waffle, a nationalist group within the social democratic New Democratic Party, which advocated for an independent Canada where a Canadian elite would replace the current U.S. masters.

Two years earlier, in 1970, Mathews demonstrated with others outside the offices of Ryerson Press, then owned by the United Church of Canada, after the announcement that it would be sold to McGraw-Hill, a U.S.-owned publisher. Ryerson Press, founded in 1920, was renowned for its educational publishing, producing materials widely used in schools across Canada. This demonstration and the consternation of writers and educators pointed out how few Canadian publishers existed. The demonstrators clearly understood that the passing of Ryerson Press to McGraw-Hill would usher in a flow of U.S. educational materials into Canada. In the end, McGraw-Hill purchased Ryerson Press, setting up a McGraw-Hill-owned company named McGraw-Hill Ryerson.

Mathews will be largely remembered as a cultural nationalist engaged in actions that attempted to protect organizations like Ryerson Press from integration with U.S. corporate interests. Yet, he was also as profoundly concerned about the economics and politics of the country as he was about its literature and culture. "Unless," said Mathews, "you control your own economy, you cannot have your own culture and it is culture which finally determines the Canadian identity."[1] For him, the two were inextricably connected.

The 1960s and 1970s were a high point in the struggle of Canadians to control their own destiny. For Mathews, the struggle was clear. It was one between the rulers and the ruled. He said, "The one group engaged in the struggle might be called the settlers and community builders. The other might be called the entrepreneurs or exploiters of land, wealth and people."[2] For him, it was undoubtedly a class struggle, and it was from a socialist perspective that he pursued his work.

Mathews insisted that the beginnings of a Canadian literary identity be nurtured by writers like John Richardson and Susanne Moodie. Richardson wrote the novel *Wacousta* in 1835. It was published by Thomas Cadell in London and William Blackwood in Edinburgh. Moodie's work *Roughing It in the Bush* was published in London in 1852. Of these writers, Mathews said, "They shared especially significant complementary roles relative to the idea of identity, the meaning of place and the sense of community."[3] While the "settlers and community builders" were engaged in a struggle with the British colonial powers for political representation, writers like Richardson and Moodie were in the nascent stage of a literature and culture that was distinct from that of their colonial masters. "*Wacousta*," says Mathews, "is at the centre of the Canadian imagination."[4]

Canadian Writers, Culture and Publishing

It took over a hundred years, but eventually, the concern of Canadians seeking a cultural identity and a vehicle for cultural expression was heard even by the state. In 1957, the John Diefenbaker government established The Canadian Council for the Arts. It was the beginning of government funding for the arts, including publishing, which has escalated over the past 66 years. While the national struggle has been an abject failure on the political and economic front, the plethora of Canadian writers who have emerged during these 66 years constructs a somewhat different story regarding Canadian culture and the publishing of Canadian writers by Canadian-owned publishers. While the

---

[1]   BC Bookworld, vol. 37, no. 3, August 2023.

[2]   Mathews, Robin. *Canadian Literature: Surrender or Revolution*. Steel Rail Educational Publishing, Toronto, 1978, p. 4.

[3]   Ibid, p. 27.

[4]   Ibid, p. 13.

vast majority of books published in Canada are published by non-Canadian publishers, Canadian writers and their Canadian publishers have made a significant dent in the onslaught of foreign books and writers published by foreign publishers.

When Canadian publishing was little known in the mid-twentieth century, it was not easy for writers to find an audience. There were few Canadian publishers, and foreign publishers were more interested in importing and selling books by foreign authors edited and printed outside Canada than they were in spotting new talent. It's vastly more expensive to do all the work of book publishing in Canada rather than importing ready-made books. Even when published by one of the few independent Canadian-owned publishers, the monetary return for an author was negligible. When Margaret Atwood's first book, *The Circle Game,* was published in Montreal by Contact Press in 1966, her remuneration was a mere 12 copies of the book.[5]

But help was forthcoming. In 1979, 22 years after the Canada Council of the Arts was founded, the federal government established the Canadian Book Publishing Development Program. In the ensuing years, the book industry support program went through two name changes. In 1986, it became the Book Publishing Industry Development Program (BPIDP). In 2010, it morphed into the Canadian Book Fund. Government propaganda told us that the name changes were a reflection of the growth of the industry. If the truth be known, the name changes were most likely politically motivated. Nevertheless, the principal objective remains: to strengthen the Canadian-owned and controlled sector of the industry and to publish and market Canadian books in both domestic and international markets.

In the mid-20th century, the Canadian-owned publishing industry consisted of a small number of companies mainly specializing in the production and publication of school textbooks. As industry insider Roy MacSkimming points out, "In the late 50s and early 60s, there might be only half a dozen first novels and no more than twenty novels in total published in a whole year....It (trade publishing) was a sideline indulged in for reasons of pride and prestige, not profit." But by the year 2000, the situation had changed. Canadian houses published 171 novels, 72 percent of the 238 novels published in Canada. In a 2017 report prepared for the ACP,[6] MacSkimming highlights how Canadian-

5   Hunt, Nick. *The Story of CanLit.* House of Anansi Press, Toronto, 2017, p. 94.
6   MacSkimming, Roy. *Net Benefit: Canada's Policy on Foreign Investment in the Book Industry.* Association of Canadian Publishers, Toronto, 2017, p. 23.

owned publishers were responsible for 80 percent of the Canadian-authored books published in Canada.

Aided by increased government funding, growth in the publication of Canadian-authored books by Canadian-owned publishers began to offset the influx of foreign titles, mainly published by firms based in the U.S. and UK. While these Canadian-owned companies were minuscule compared to the large foreign companies, Canadians, for the first time, had a genuine choice to buy and read Canadian authors, to read about Canada from the point of view of Canadians. At the same time, Canadian authors who published with branch plant publishers often were first published by small Canadian publishers. It was those small, struggling Canadian companies that initially put many authors on the map and even made them household names.

When the Independent Publishers Association (IPA) was founded in 1973, it had 16 members. In 2022, the IPA's successor, the Association of Canadian Publishers (ACP), included 115 Canadian-owned companies. A 2018 report prepared for the ACP by Nordcity identified 245 active English-language Canadian-owned publishers; of these, 78 percent had less than ten employees.[7] It was these small companies that published the first books of many Canadian authors. Today, only four percent of books published in Canada are published by Canadian-owned houses, yet that small percentage continues to exert a resounding echo across the nation.

This four percent would undoubtedly be higher if Canadian writers, who were first introduced to the world by a Canadian-owned publisher, would consider publishing not just their first but also subsequent books with a Canadian-owned publisher, as Mathews chose to do.

The Struggle for Canadian Universities

In the 1960s and 1970s, there was both a dearth of Canadian content and Canadian professors in this country's universities. For many studying English literature at a Canadian university, there was no Canadian content. Still, writers, playwrights and publishers emerged with a strong voice that was heard across the country. It was in the hard-fought battle for Canadian identity where Mathews made what may have been his most significant contribution. Yet, there were multiple dimensions to Mathews' contribution to developing

---

[7]   Nordcity, p. 8.

a Canadian cultural identity. Most were hard-won battles where he refused to give up.

Much of the literature Canadians read in the early 60s was massively influenced and modelled on British and, increasingly, American writing. Mathews postulated that Canadian literature, sparse as it was in the mid-20th century, was uniquely Canadian, unique at least when compared to British and U.S. imperialist literature, which was being foisted on the Canadian people. Most themes of U.S. literature were centred around the heroic individual. In contrast, Mathews, tracing this theme back to *Wacousta*, posited that much of the literature written in Canada, what he would consider true Canadian literature, was primarily about community, about people working together, and about nature. "The philosophy of community in Canada," wrote Mathews, "has been different from the United States right from the beginning....We have chosen not to be part of the most powerful empire in history, though it has colonized us through our ruling class".[8] Canadian writers wishing to create a distinct literature fought against this individually orientated literature. Yet, the lure of American writing was compelling for many Canadian writers for whom success only came — or so they thought — when they were recognized by the U.S. literary establishment. Such literature would be framed in this individualistic model, which the U.S. literary establishment saw as superior to all others and the model which determined greatness. All other literature, including Canadian, was wanting. The struggle for a Canadian identity could be likened to an ant struggling with an elephant. The struggle for space against the onslaught of U.S. culture was stressful and consuming. Yet, as more space for Canadian creators emerged, the variance between Canadian and U.S. culture, so elegantly described by Mathews, became more apparent.

Mathews knew that if Canadian culture and Canadian writing were to have a prominent place in this country, there had to be a strong Canadian presence among the teaching staff in Canadian universities and educational institutions. The 1968 publication of *The Struggle for Canadian Universities*, edited by Mathews and James Steele, both professors of literature at Carleton University, launched a national campaign for the Canadianization of Canadian universities. This book brought to the fore the fact that there was a minority of Canadians employed as academics in Canadian universities. As a result, all too many of the courses taught at Canadian universities, particularly in the Social Sciences and Humanities, came out of the cultural

---

[8] Mathews, Robin. 1978, p. 3.

experience and education of non-Canadian professors. They came to teach in Canada until they could get an academic position back home. But they didn't teach about Canada. The situation was dismal. For example, Professor J. Lawrence Black observed that in 1969, Laurentian University's Political Science department offered only a half-course in Canadian government. Its Geography department offered no courses in Canadian geography; likewise, its English department offered no courses in Canadian literature. But thanks, in large part, to Mathews and Steele, this was all to change.

The campaign launched by Mathews and Steele at Carleton University became known as the Canadianization campaign or the Canadianization Movement. With the 1969 publication of *The Struggle for Canadian Universities*, Mathews and Steele launched a movement across Canada to increase the number of Canadian citizens teaching in Canadian universities. The movement did not start with a bang. Mathews and Steele first asked Carleton University to ensure that, when hiring new professors, Canadian citizens would eventually form a two-thirds majority of faculty. They further recommended, before the appointment of a non-Canadian, a vacancy was to be well advertised in this country. In addition, they asked that Canadian citizenship be made a necessary qualification for all future appointments to administrative positions. When the recommendations were put before the Carleton University Academic Staff Association, the reception was dismal. One colleague even attempted to present a motion to refer Mathews and Steele to the Ontario Human Rights Commission, suggesting that they should be criminally charged. The motions presented by Mathews and Steele "were defeated by a vote of 138 to 5.[9]

However, the response from across the country was enormous and largely favourable. At the same time, Mathews wrote fiction, non-fiction and he wrote poetry. Yes, he was a university professor. But Mathews also knew that little would be achieved if his writing and teaching were not combined and backed up with action. If the Canadianization movement was to bear fruit, a bold, aggressive and popular plan of action needed to be devised.

As a result, Mathews and Steele, never ones to rest on their laurels, launched a Canada-wide campaign to change university hiring practices across the country. Largely at their own expense, they travelled across the country, speaking at more than 20 universities in all provinces except Prince Edward Island. Between 1970 and 1980, through the work of scholars across

---

9   Mathews, Robin, and James Steele. *The Struggle for Canadian Universities.* New Press, Toronto, 1969, p. 7.

the country and pressure from concerned students active in campus radio, campus newspapers, and student organizations, the Canadian content in Canadian university courses increased significantly. Responding to the wide-ranging debate and the growing concern over the inadequate study of Canadian matters in many disciplines, the Association of Universities and Colleges in Canada (AUCC) —an organization of university executive heads representing their respective institutions— decided to consider the question of Canadian resources for teaching Canadian content. In 1972, just four years after Mathews and Steele published their seminal book, the AUCC commissioned T.H.B. Symons, president of Trent University, to commence a study of university curriculum and hiring practices. The report, widely known as the "Symons Report," was released in 1976 under the title *To Know Ourselves. The Report of the Commission on Canadian Studies.* Mathews essentially saw Symons as a "sell-out" and said:

> Spokesmen and managers in the culture fill the same role as sell-outs and their counterparts in politics and the economy. T.H.B. Symons ...appears to have been picked because he was a nationalist seriously concerned with survival and self-determination. Perhaps he thought he was. But the A.U.C.C. ... spent a few years seeking a 'suitable' commissioner. They found one in Tom Symons. The commission was struck in 1972. It was awarded $350,000.00. It had used free and voluntary help from coast to coast. Its first bloodless and banal report was two years late. Its most important report — on personnel, hiring, hiring practices, origin of faculty, and 'adaptability' of foreign faculty — is nowhere in sight.

Despite such shenanigans, the Canadianization campaign spread beyond academia, touching the hearts and minds of many Canadians. The furor Mathews raised caught the attention of the Federal Government. The sentiment across the country meant that government could no longer allow the continued colonization of Canadian universities. To do so would be a kind of political suicide. Consequently, in 1977, the Department of Manpower and Immigration introduced rules to ensure fairer hiring practices at Canadian universities. In 1977, it made advertising in Canada mandatory for all academic vacancies. In 1981, it stipulated that a search for Canadian applicants would be necessary before it would approve a job offer to a foreign candidate. Many academics, particularly foreign administrators, found it difficult to give unqualified priority to Canadians. The Canadian Association of University Teachers, while supporting the idea of advertising, asserted that competence should be the principal criterion for employing both Canadian and foreign scholars. They, of course, never defined the criteria that determined competence. Was the ability to teach Canadian students about their own country part of that criteria? For Mathews and Steele, it was. For purists, the issue of competence became a defence against hiring Canadians. Yet the Canadianization campaign bore fruit.

In 2006, when Steele and Mathews surveyed the calendar description of courses in five disciplines at six universities for the years 1970, 1975, and 1980, they found that by 1975, the number of courses listing Canadian content had increased by 75 percent and that such courses had doubled by 1980.

Beyond the University

Robin Mathews believed Canadian literature was unique. More specifically, he regarded it as distinct from American literature. He asserted, "The Canadian and foreign operating class have never been very much interested in the participation of the Canadian people in the organization of national life."[10] "The other people - the great majority — are the settlers and community builders, who have wanted to make Canada the primary place for Canadians."[11] For Mathews, it was not only a question of increasing the number of Canadian professors. For him, it was also important, and possibly more crucial, that the content of courses focus on what he considered to be unique to Canadian literature and Canadians in general. Like all good advocates, Mathews believed Canadian cultural expression was superior to that of its southern neighbour.

Mathews' activism spanned the spectrum of society, seeking to bring to the "settlers and community builders" an enhanced understanding of Canada and its unique culture. He was never satisfied and always sought to build new platforms for propagating Canadian culture and interpretations. Doing so meant moving out into the wider society, away from academia, to work with others to establish institutions for disseminating Canadian culture. In 1975, Robin participated with others to found a theatre company, The Great Canadian Theatre Company (GCTC) (See Bill Law's essay, "The Great Canadian Theatre Company: In the Beginning" in this edition) in Ottawa and a publishing company, Steel Rail Educational Publishing (SREP) in Toronto.

---

[10] Mathews, Robin. *Canadian Literature: Surrender or Revolution*. Steel Rail Educational Publishing, Toronto, p. 169.
[11] Ibid, p. 4.

Robin and Esther Mathews joined the author, Greg Keilty, Edith Hemery and Olino Capacchione, estranged employees of the Canadian Liberation Movement's NC Press, and the poet Milton Acorn, to establish Steel Rail Educational Publishing (SREP). During the next ten years, Robin published four books with Steel Rail, including *Canadian Literature: Surrender or Revolution*, in which he brought together a collection of essays that carefully presented his thesis on Canadian culture and Canadian literature. In the preface to *Canadian Literature*, Gail Dexter says this book "points to those fundamental qualities of the collective experience that uniquely characterize Canadian life, and therefore Canadian letters."[12] While Dexter's effervescence about Canadian uniqueness may be overstated, it was this foundation on which Robin Mathews and a plethora of groups and individuals built their case for a unique Canadian identity. There is no doubt: Robin Mathews was a key figure in emphasizing the necessity for Canadians to articulate a comprehensive understanding that would be crucial to fabricating a common identity. However, to fabricate a common identity, all people need to be included.

Assessing the National Movement

As the national movement grew, the spectrum of groups promulgating a nationalist politics for Canada broadened. Included in this spectrum, were the Centrist social democrats, the NDP and the Waffle, The Committee for an Independent Canada (1975), The Council of Canadians (1985) and the National Party of Canada (1992). Mel Hurtig, who founded Hurtig Publishing in 1972 in Edmonton, was a key figure. Among the many achievements of Hurtig Publishing was the publication of the three-volume *The Canadian Encyclopedia* in 1985 and The *Junior Encyclopedia of Canada* in 1990. On the far left, groups like the Canadian Liberation Movement (CLM) advocated for independent Canadian Unions and an independent socialist Canada. With the exception of CLM and a few other small left-leaning groups who, at least rhetorically, advocated for an independent socialist Canada, the mainstream of the national movement primarily sought to wrest control of the economy, the state, and cultural expression from the hands of what Mathews called the "entrepreneurs and exploiters of land, wealth and people." As Mathews saw it, the operating class was an alliance between the foreign imperialists and Canadian compradors.

---

[12]   Ibid, p. 5.

"The operating class," said Mathews, "has won the largest share of power...Our resources are largely foreign-owned. Our culture is heavily foreign-dominated. Our economy is fundamentally a staples economy. Canada does not possess an independent foreign policy, nor does it have a population of workers represented by its own trade unions."[13] It must be noted that the foreign exploiters had willing and helpful allies among Canadian compradors who hitched their wagons to the engine of foreign imperialists. Mathews, himself, always seeking new avenues to promote Canadian nationalism, jumped into the political fray as the leader of the National Party of Canada formed in 1979. He ran for office in Ottawa Centre. (The party that Mathews co-founded should not be confused with the national party Mel Hurtig founded thirteen years later.) Mathews was a socialist. At least for a time, he worked with other left-leaning organizations. Hurtig was a nationalist, not a socialist. While Mathews was keenly aware of the class, gender and racist structures that dominated Canadian society, Hurtig and others of his persuasion were what might be called bourgeois nationalists. They wanted independence for Canada in the shape of a class-structured society where the "settlers and community builders" played second fiddle to the bourgeois nationalists.[14]

Overall, the independence movement, in all its configurations, paid little attention to the maligned, exploited, and murdered Indigenous people within their midst. The Indigenous people were largely relegated to reserves and other marginal places in society.

In the U.S., Howard W. French points out that it was "slave-owning whites themselves who claimed to be victims of slavery to Britain because of their lack of political representation, and when push came to shove, they fought a revolution in order to secure what they called their freedom."[15] In Canada, a somewhat different route emerged. Canadian nationalism, for the most part, took a more peaceful, all be it a more convoluted path to independence, one that involved primarily white people and 'their liberation.' With the passage of the Constitution Act in 1982, 115 years after the signing of the British North American Act, Canada gained, at least, nominal and quasi-legal independence from Britain. Yet, questions

---

[13]   Ibid, p. XII.
[14]   Ibid, p. 5.
[15]   French, Howard. *Born in Blackness: Africa, Africans and the Making of the Modern World, 1471 to the Second World War.* Liverlight Publishing, New York, 2021, p. 330.

remained unanswered. Who exactly were the settler and community builders that Mathews discussed?

The settlers were, for the most part, people seeking to escape the oppression that rained upon them in their home country. Among them were the highland Scots, who had been left destitute after the highland clearances, and the Irish fleeing the Irish famine. The people's struggles, the independence movement as a whole, were firmly rooted in a Euro-centric worldview. While Mathews himself saw "native values expressed through the land and Indigenous people"[16] as a critical component in building a Canadian identity, the vision of a society based on community and native values was overwhelmingly absent from most nationalist rhetoric. Indigenous people were seen, when they were seen at all, as somewhat nebulous participants in white people's struggles. Indigenous cultures, Indigenous ways of seeing, and Indigenous world views, like those of so many subjected people, were seldom part of the dialogue. While the white settlers sought independence from Britain, the Indian Act, the main goal of which was to compel Indigenous people to forsake their culture and embrace the dominant Euro-centric culture of white Canadians, was passed into law in 1876, nine years after the British North American Act came into existence. Canadian nationalists only engaged with Indigenous people when the support of Indigenous people and many oppressed people aligned with their goals. White settler Canadians assume that their fight for independence was less brutal than in the United States. Indigenous people might beg to differ. The Canadian national movement, with the exception of socialist advocates like Mathews, was never about them. It, like in the United States, was about white settlers seeking independence from imperial Britain and, in the case of Canada, imperialist domination of the U.S.

A poignant illustration of this is brilliantly portrayed by Zebedee Nungak in his book *Wrestling with Colonialism on Steroids: Québec Inuit Fight for their Homeland.* In 1912, the Canadian Federal government ceded the northern part of what is now Québec to the Québec provincial government. After 1912, the province ignored the territory for 52 years. In 1964, the Québec provincial government, awakened by and in support of the James Bay Hydro Electric Project, moved into the territory on mass. Premier Jean Lesage sent his minister of natural resources, René Lévesque, to meet with Inuit

---

16   Mathews, Robin. *Canadian Literature: Surrender or Revolution.* Steel Rail Educational Publishing, Toronto, 1978, p. 6.

leaders to let them know that Québec was here from now on. In 1968, Lévesque became the leader of the newly formed Parti Québécois. The Parti Québécois and leader René Lévesque, while deeply engaged in a struggle for Québec independence and sovereignty, had little stomach for affording the Inuit the same opportunity. In fact, the Inuit had control of their land from 1912-1964. When the Québec government moved in, first under the liberals, then under the separatist Parti Québécois, they imposed the French language, French names, and French culture on the Inuit. Zabadee Nungak tells us that "The content and substance of Québec does not at all exist in Inuit traditions."[17] Like their counterparts in English Canada, the Québec nationalists had no interest in promoting or supporting Inuit traditions. The thought of listening to or even including a discussion of Indigenous thought and philosophy was an enigma.

Conclusion

Mathews' concept of "community builders" pointed to a more holistic, less stratified society than most interpretations, much like the one described above by Zebedee Nungak. His vision was based on an inclusive understanding of Canada. When Robin spoke of "native values expressed through the land and Indigenous people" and "community builders," he envisioned a different society, one that included all people, including Indigenous people, who occupied the lower rungs of the social hierarchy. Had this understanding been included in a more meaningful way in the independence movement, a clearer understanding of a more open and free society, a society that saw humans as part of rather than conquerers of nature, could have emerged. While Mathews is best known for his struggle for Canadian universities, to see Mathews in this singularity would be to do him and that for which he fought a great injustice. Karl Marx said in 1844, "The statement that the physical and mental life of man, and nature, are interdependent means simply that nature is interdependent with itself, for man is a part of nature." Mathews' vision was inclusive, not narrowly focused on one goal or objective. In his own words: "The angry struggle for the universities is only one of the manifestations of unease about survival and self-determination."

---

17   Nungak, Zebedee. *Wrestling With Colonialism on Steroids: Québec Inuit Fight for Their Homeland.* Montréal: Véhicule Press, 2017, p. 39.

Works Cited

BC Bookworld, vol. 37, no. 3, August 2023.

French, Howard. *Born in Blackness: Africa, Africans and the Making of the Modern World, 1471 to the Second World War*, Liverlight Publishing: New York, 2021.

Hunt, Nick. *The Story of CanLit*. House of Anansi Press, Toronto, 2017.

MacSkimming, Roy. *Net Benefit: Canada's Policy on Foreign Investment in the Book Industry*. Association of Canadian Publishers, Toronto, 2017.

Mathews, Robin. *Canadian Literature: Surrender or Revolution*. Steel Rail Educational Publishing, Toronto, 1978.

Mathews, Robin and James Steele. *The Struggle for Canadian Universities*. New Press, Toronto, 1969.

Nordcity, *The Canadian English Language Book Publishing Industry Profile; Final Report*. Toronto, Association of Canadian Publishers, 2018.

Nungak, Zebedee. *Wrestling With Colonialism on Steroids: Québec Inuit Fight for Their Homeland*. Véhicule Press, Montréal, 2017.